Dharma in the Hindu Ethics
With special reference to the Mahābhārata

Dharma in the Hindu Ethics

With special reference to the Mahābhārata

By:

Birendra Prasad Mishra

Formerly Chairperson, Philosophy & Sanskrit Instruction Committee,
Tri - Chandra Multiple Campus, Kathmandu, Nepal

ADROIT

Adroit Publishers

NEW DELHI • KATHMANDU

ISBN : 978-81-87393-43-6

2019

Published by
ADROIT PUBLISHERS 4675/21, Ganpati Bhawan, Ansari Road,
Daryaganj, New Delhi-110 002, INDIA, Phone : 011-23266030
adroitpublishers@gmail.com

Typeset in URW Palladio CSX+ by Arun Sharma,
Akriti Graphic Solution, Delhi-110081 E-mail: arun263923@gmail.com,
Ph: 9999414390

Dedicated to:

The memory of my uncle Ram Narayan Mishra from whom I received blessings and perennial inspirations.

Preface

The purview of the Hindu ethics is vast. It is extremely difficult if not impossible to include all matters related to it in a small book like this. The book does not pretend to be the only book on the subject. It is an attempt to present before the reader a systematic and synthetic view of the Hindu ethics based primarily on the great epic, the Mahābhārata.

During the limited period of research, I tried to go deeply into the Hindu ethics which was chiefly instrumental in the preservation of the Hindu organization. Hinduism is not only a religion but a mode of life and as such is spread over to several parts of the globe. India, the biggest Hindu dwelling country in the world, although declared secular by the constitution remains predominantly Hindu. Hinduism, as is known, has never been rigid, hence always been dynamic in its approach, absorbing all those races which invaded the Hindu culture from time to time. It is somewhat a mystery as well as a matter of pride that despite several invasions and prolonged domination and ruling by foreign invaders, Hinduism has continued to sustain and inspire. No doubt, in course of thousands of years, there have taken place certain developments which divided the Hindu society and affected its cultural, religious and social fibres.

It is imperative, therefore, to be profound and well informed with the Hindu ethics so that an insight into the present situation could be gained. For, I have always believed that it is only in the light of the past the present can be understood and improved.

Previously, Nepal was the only Hindu kingdom in the world. However, with the people's movement of 2006 against the king, the elected Constituent Assembly adopted the new constitution that declared Nepal a Secular Federal Democratic Republic state on September 20, 2015. Since then, Nepal ceased to exist as a Hindu kingdom.

This book, it is hoped, will be useful for those who teach philosophy in different universities at different levels as well as to the students who in higher studies pursue philosophy in general and ethics in particular. Common readers will also be found to be benefitted from the book.

In the new edition, the strength of the book is that it puts flesh on the bare bones of the thesis that was approved for the degree of Ph.D. by the University of Patna in 1968. I was a recipient of the scholarship provided by the Government of India under the Technical Cooperation Scheme of the Colombo plan. I wish to express my gratitude to Prof. Hari Mohan Jha, Head of the Department of Philosophy, Patna University from whom I obtained valuable guidance. I will be failing in my duty if I do not acknowledge the help I received from Prof. Girish Prasad Singh of English Department of Tri-Chandra Campus, Kathmandu, Nepal who had taken considerable trouble in correcting the language of the book. I thank Mr. Akhil Sharma of Adroit Publishers, Darya Ganj, New Delhi, for printing the book. I am thankful to Er. Ganesh Khania for checking the proofs of the book. At last, I thank all those whose help has facilitated the publication of the book.

I am afraid that there are many errors and defects in the book that have been left uncorrected and for those, I crave the indulgence of the reader.

- Birendra Prasad Mishra

92/22, Miteri Marg, Old Baneshwor,
Kathmandu-31, Nepal.
E-mail-mishra_bp@yahoo.com

Transliteration Chart

अ आ इ ई उ ऊ ऋ
a ā i ī u ū ṛ

ए ऐ ओ औ
è ai o ao

क ख ग घ ङ
ka kha ga gha ṅa

च छ ज झ ञ
ca cha ja jha ña

ट ठ ड ढ ण
ṭa ṭha ḍa ḍha ṇa

त थ द ध न
ta tha da dha na

प फ ब भ म
pa pha ba bha ma

व र ल ब श ष स ह
ya ra la va śa ṣa sa ha

श्र त्र ज्ञ ँ : ऽ
kṣa tra jña ṁ ḥ ,

Abbreviations

Ādi.	—	Ādiparva.
Sabhā	—	Sabhāparva.
Vana.	—	Vanaparva.
Virāṭa.	—	Virāṭaparva.
Udyoga	—	Udyogaparva.
Bhīṣma	—	Bhīṣmaparva.
Droṇa	—	Droṇaparva.
Karṇa.	—	Karṇaparva.
Śalya.	—	Śalyaparva.
Sauptika.	—	Sauptikaparva.
Strī.	—	Strīparva.
Śānti.	—	Śāntiparva.
Anuśā (Anu)	—	Anuśāsanaparva.
Āśva.	—	Āśvamedhikaparva.
Āśrama	—	Āśramavāsikaparva
Mausala	—	Mausalaparva
Mahaāpra.	—	Mahāprasthānikaparva.
Svargā.	—	Svargārohaṇaparva.
Bāla.	—	Bālakāṇḍa.

Ayodhyā(Ayo.)	—	Ayodhyākāṇḍa.
Araṇya	—	Araṇyakāṇḍa.
Kiṣ	—	Kiṣkindhākāṇḍa.
Sund.	—	Sundarakāṇḍa.
Laṁkā.	—	Laṁkākāṇḍa.
Uttar.	—	Uttarkāṇḍa.
Gītā	—	Bhagavadgītā

Contents

	Preface	*vii*
	Abbreviations	*ix*
	Introduction	*1*
1.	The Notion of Dharma	11
2.	Social and Individual Ethics	54
3.	Political Ethics	84
4.	The Problem of Fate and Free Will	110
5.	The Different Standards of Morality	129
6.	Summary and Conclusion	172
	Bibliography	187

Introduction

The ethics of the Hindus is not meant for the Hindus alone, as the very title suggests. It stands for all human beings irrespective of their faith. It is common or general in nature. Ethics, a normative science of the conduct of human beings living in societies, is generally considered as a system of moral principles or rules of behaviour of human beings. Therefore, it is applicable to all and at all times. Its purview is broad as it encompasses material, moral, biological and spiritual goals (Puruṣartha) of all human endeavours. Significantly, it is not confined to only one source for its origin. Its roots are traceable to the Vedas, the Brāhmaṇas, the Upaniṣads, the Smṛtis and epics like the Rāmāyaṇa and the Mahābhārata.

The Rāmāyaṇa and the Mahābhārata are the real depositories of the ancient eternal (Sanātana) culture. Especially, the Mahābhārata contains all knowledge and information of its age. The epic's main story was written much later than the events narrated took place. Many interpolations into the main text have made the epic bulky. The epic is called the Mahābhārata not because of its weight or its voluminous shape but on account of the battle of morals or ideals that was preached by the saints and seers and practised by the masses and the privileged personalities of the then Bhārata nation (Bhāratavarṣa). Even today, every conscientious individual fights his inner battle while taking his final decision as to what ought to be done when two alternatives are before him. Perhaps, in the context of the universality of the mental conflict, the epic has been so named.

In this book an attempt has been made to study the ethics of the Hindus with special reference to the great epic, the Mahābhārata. The ethical elements are profusely interspersed in the social, political, religious and philosophical contexts of the epic. The epic has been studied by both oriental and occidental scholars with varied interests. Most of the scholars like Oldenburg, Sorensen, Hopkins, Webber, Winternitz, Holtzmann, Held, Schroeder, Barth, Pischel and Jacobi have concerned themselves with the literature and the history of the composition of the epic. There are scholars like N. V. Thadani, Ludwig Lassen and Dahlmann who have approached the epic altogether from different angles. N. V. Thadani in his book 'The Mystery of the Mahābhārata' recognizes the epic to be the symbolization of the six systems of the Hindu Philosophy and their conflict. He rejects the moral teachings of the epic when he states, "From the beginning to the very end stronger and extraordinary events take place, and not a few of them shock the moral sense and tend to dull and deaden the higher sensibility in man."[1] Ludwig interprets the epic symbolically on the basis of a nature myth. In the seasonal myth of Ludwig, the Pāṇḍavas symbolize the seasons, and Draupadī, their common spouse, is the dark earth possessed alternately by the five seasons.[2] Lassen explains it through another symbolic interpretation. The characters of the epic are not ordinary human beings. They are to be understood rather as historical conditions or circumstances.[3]

According to Dr. Sukthankar, the Mahābhārata appeared to Joseph Dahlmann above all as a treatise on jurisprudence (Dharmaśāstra). It was composed with the avowed and exclusive object of expounding all the different aspects of Hindu Law, in the widest sense of the term not omitting even its historical and archaic features and oddities.[4] He had denied historical reality to the fable and toyed with the idea of symbolism. The polyandrous marriage especially, according to Dahlmann, was but a symbol of the perfect unity of the Hindu joint family. The battle as depicted in the epic took place only in the imagination of the poet.[5] K. M. Munshi takes the epic more comprehensively. To him, "The Mahābhārata is not a mere epic; it is a romance, telling the tale of heroic men and women and of some who were divine; it is a whole literature in itself, containing a code of life; a philosophy of social and ethical relations, and speculative thought on human problems that is hard to rival; but above all, it has for its core the Gītā, which is, as the world is beginning to find out, the noblest of scriptures and the grandest of sagas in which the climax is reached in the wondrous Apocalypse in the Eleventh Canto."[6] According to C. Rajagopalachari, the epic has been influencing the character and civilization of the major population of the world since time immemorial. He maintains, "The Mahābhārata has moulded the character and civilization of one of the most numerous of the world's people. How did it fulfil-how is it still continuing to fulfil-this function? By its gospel of dharma, which like a golden thread runs through all the complex movements in the epic; by its lesson that hatred breeds hatred, that covetousness and violence lead inevitably to ruin, that the only real conquest is in the battle against one's lower nature."[7] Aurobindo also regards moral issues as the main aim of the writer of the epic. He remarks, "His (Vyāsa's) deep preoccupation with the ethical issues of speech and action is very notable. His very subject is one of practical ethics, the establishment of a Dharmarājya, an empire of the just, by which is meant no millennium of the saints, but the practical ideal of government with righteousness, purity and unselfish toil for the common good as its saving principles."[8] About the aim of the epic, C. V. Vaidya observes, "That the Mahābhārata was made the vehicle of moral and religious instruction is so apparent that it hardly requires any proof. In fact, the work has almost lost its character as an epic poem and has become, and has always been acknowledged as a Smriti and a Dharmashastra."[9] Vyāsa's message through the medium of the epic is supposed to be the maintenance of righteousness and holiness, truthfulness and so on. In this connection, K. S. Ramaswami Sastri observes, "The supreme world message of Vyasa is the eternal message of all the sages and saints and seers and of all the world-faiths in the universe viz., righteousness and holiness."[10]

The epic has been regarded as a 'moral encyclopedia' by A. A. MacDonell[11] and as 'encyclopedia of Indian culture' by K. S. Ramaswami Sastri.[12] Monier Williams also regards it as the cyclopaedia of ethics, philosophy and history. He observes, "The great epic, however, is not so much a poem with a single subject as a vast cyclopaedia or thesaurus of Hindu mythology, legendary, history, ethics and, philosophy."[13] Shravaka says, "The epic is also designated as Nitishastra-code of morality; how men and women of all ages, different castes and classes, various stages and statures should behave."[14]

P. L. Vaidya, accepting the later interpolations in the epic concerning ethics, observes, "These assertions do not, however, alter the total character of the Mahābhārata, because in its final form it combines in itself the characteristics of several śāstras, including those of Nīti, Mokṣa, Dharma, Artha and Kāma. The Mahābhārata is indeed a Dharmaśāstra par excellence, presenting, as it does, systematic law and general morality."[15] As it mainly deals with the moral concept of Dharma, it is called Dharmaśāstra. He further states, "Dharma represents not only the foundation on which the whole stately edifice of the Mahābhārata has been erected, but also, to a great extent, its material. The character of the Mahābhārata as a Dharma-śāstra, or Smṛti, will be evident from the three main divisions of the Smṛtis, as seen in the discourses on Varṇāśrama-dharma, or ācāra, śrāddha, dāyabhāga, or vyavahāra, prāyascitta, and the rest."[16]

Thus the Mahābhārata is not merely a narrative of battles, but is predominantly didactic in character. Though the ethical principles are scattered in most of the parvas, they are more elaborately expounded in the Vana, Udyoga, Bhīśma, Śānti and Anuśāsana parvas. The author has tried to convey his ethical teachings through a very interesting story of the battle to impress upon the minds of children, youths and old men. This has been done to keep these moral preachings alive for centuries to influence and mould human understanding and behaviour.

The story of the Mahābhārata is not a complex one. It states a fierce fighting between the Kauravas and the Pāṇḍavas, the cousins, for the lofty throne of Hastināpur. These two parties fought for eighteen days with eighteen akṣauhiṇis of soldiers in the battle-field of Kurukṣetra. In the battle, the Pāṇḍavas, who were the rightful owner of the throne came out victorious. The story states that even the mightier warriors like Bhīśma, Droṇa, Karṇa were on the side of the Kauravas, but they were defeated by the Pāṇḍavas who were less in number, and were supported by Kṛṣṇa, who has been given divine status in the epic.

The very defeat of the mightier Kauravas stands for nothing but the defeat of injustice by justice, and of Adharma by Dharma. Here lies the ethical significance of the epic. The battle symbolizes the battle between ethical and unethical ends, between fair and unfair means, between justified claim and unjustified claim. The Kauravas were defeated because their motive was impure and malicious, and they tried to occupy the throne which legitimately belonged to the Pāṇḍavas. The Kauravas were wrong from the very beginning when they wanted to acquire the throne and to banish the Pāṇḍavas. For this unjustified end, they adopted wrong means like playing the game of dice. Even in the play, they were not fair which resulted in the defeat of the eldest brother, who lost everything including his common wife and throne and received banishment for thirteen years. The Kauravas committed wrongs one after another. They tried to denude Draupadī, the lady of the same family, but failed. She was rescued by Kṛṣṇa. They did not stop there but went far ahead on the path of injustice. After the return of the Pāṇḍavas from banishment, the Kauravas did not return the kingdom to them. The Pāṇḍavas were ready to satisfy themselves even with five villages as their own share in the kingdom. But the Kauravas were not in a mood to give an inch of land to them. All these necessarily led to the disastrous war which destroyed all the Kauravas along with their supporters and none survived except their blind father and mother. In the battle not even a single Pāṇḍava (among the five brothers) was killed.

Along with the main stream of the story, which establishes the ethical supremacy over unethical ends, there are other small and big discourses and dialogues which throw ample light on moral issues. In this connection, the names of the Bhāgavagītā, Maṅkigītā, Bodhyagītā, Parāśaragītā Haṁsagītā Kāmagītā, and Anugītā are worth mentioning. Each of them is a discourse with an ideal. The Bhāgavadgītā has been narrated by Kṛṣṇa Himself to Arjuna who was not prepared to fight against his relatives and preceptors. In it, Kṛṣṇa preaches the patha of Jñānayoga, Karmayoga and Bhaktiyoga. In the Maṅkigītā, the casting off of the desire has been preached. At one place it observes, "One is sure to obtain happiness according to the measure of the desires he may be able to cast off. Truly, he who yields himself up to desires always suffers misery."[17] In the Bodhyagītā, saint Bodhya regards freedom from hope as high felicity and the ascetic life as the best life.[18] In the Parāśaragītā, we find elaborate discussion on the social and individual ethics.[19] In the Haṁsagītā, Brahmā explains the different aspects of ethics.[20] Again, in the Kāmagītā, the casting off of the desire has been stressed by Kṛṣṇa.[21] In the Anugītā also, the law of Karma has been enunciated and the different paths leading to Mokṣa have been suggested by Kṛṣṇa to Arjuna.[22] In the Brāhmaṇagītā, the nature of the Brahman and the ways of self-realisation have been pointed out by the learned Brāhmin to his wife.[23]

Apart from these Gītās which deal mainly with the ethical issues, there are many significant dialogues and discourses as between the bird Pūjanī and the King Brahmadatta,[24] between the cat Lomaśa and the rat Palita,[25] between the butcher and Visvāmitra,[26] between the hunter and the pigeon[27] and others.

In the epic, there are several occasions on which issues of various nature have been raised and discussed. The aim of the epic is mainly to deal with the ethical issues. The whole epic stands on the pillars of morality as ethical questions are involved almost at every stage of the story.

It is quite obvious that the outstanding characters in the epic represent different virtues and vices. The life of Bhīṣma may be said to represent a deep regard for truth and duty. Yudhiṣṭhira stands for truth and honesty. He is regarded as the most virtuous character in the epic. Arjuna stands for bravery, Vidura, for wisdom and Droṇa for an ideal preceptor. Duryodhana, the eldest of the Kauravas, is a symbol of unscrupulous and insatiate greed for political power. The King Dhṛatrāṣṭra stands for egoistic self, who always worries for his own sons, who are unjust. He never bothers about his nephews, who are just and right. Draupadī represents the ideal virtuous house-wife. Karṇa stands for a faithful friend who does not favour even his own mother and brothers and gives his life for the sake of friendship. He does not betray his faithful friend Duryodhana. Thus, almost all characters represent special virtues and vices for which they stand in the epic.

This book aims at a critical study of the Hindu ethics in general and the ethical ideas in the Mahābhārata in particular. The whole work has been divided into six chapters. In the first chapter, the notion of 'Dharma' has been discussed in detail. 'Dharma' is used in a wide sense including the different aspects of morality, spiritualism, and political values.

A separate chapter has been devoted to discuss the Varnāṣrama Dharmas which occupied an important place in the age of the epic. In the epic period, society was divided into four varṇas or classes and the life of a man was categorised under four āśramas or stages, each with its specific obligations.

The duties and rights of a man are determined by the state, which safeguards the interests of the individuals and communities with a view to securing and promoting their well-being. So, political morality has been dealt with in a separate chapter.

Some of the characters in the epic are found to have a deep faith in fate and some of them have a sincere regard for human endeavour. Naturally, the problem of fate and free will has been discussed in a separate chapter.

Different standards of morality have been pointed out in the epic in various contexts. Among them, the theory of hedonism, the theory of self-conquest, the theory of self-realisation, the theory of social good, behaviour of the great men and purity of motive deserve special mention. They have been discussed in a separate chapter. The last chapter deals with the different conclusions which have been derived from the study.

Before coming over to the main issues, it would be better to write a few words about the sources which have been used in course of the research work. The different editions of the Mahābhārata have been used as the primary sources of the work. Maximum help has been taken from the Gītā Press publication of the Mahābbārata and from the Critical edition of the Bhandarkar Oriental Research Institute, Poona. As regards the English version, P. C. Roy's english translation of the epic has been utilised.

The central teaching of the epic is to establish the rule of Dharma in the world to help individuals and the community to live together in peace and tranquillity, and to make man realise the supreme goal of life. It tries to impress upon our mind that truth must prevail ultimately and that the just cause will certainly be vindicated. As C. V. Vaidya observes, "The observance of Dharma, under any condition or in any adversity, is the duty which the Mahābhārata tries constantly to inculcate through out its length."[28] Thus Dharma is the central point of the great epic. Naturally it will be proper to start with the study of Dharma.

Reference

1. Thadani, N. V., The Mystery of the Mahābhārata, Vol. III, Pt. II, p. 310.
2. Sukthankar, V. S., On the Meaning of the Mahābhārata p. 26
3. Ibid., p.26.
4. Ibid., p.23.
5. Ibid., p. 25.
6. Munshi, K. M., General Editor's Preface to The Mahābhārata by C. Rajagopalachari, p.5
7. Rajagopalachari, C., the Mahābhārata, p. 10.
8. Aurobindo, Vyāsa and Vālmiki, P. 40.
9. Vaidya, C. V., The Mahābhārata a Criticism, p. 22.
10. Sastri, K. S. Ramaswami, A Mahābhārata Primer, p. 107
11. MacDonell, A. A., India's Past, p. 88.
12. Sastri, K. S. Ramaswami, A Mahābhārata Primer, p. 2.
13. Williams, Monier, Indian Wisdom, p. 371.

14. Shravaka, Thus have I heard a living epic, Pub. in 'The Aryan Path,' Vols, 28, June, 1957; p. 243.
15. Vaidya, P. L., The Mahābhārata, its history and character, Pub, in the 'The Cultural heritage of India,' Vol. II p. 67.
16. Ibid.
17. Śānti, 177, 48.
18. Śānti, Chap. 178.
19. Śānti, Chap. 279 (cri. edi.); 290 to 298 (G. P.).
20. Śanti, Chap. 299.
21. Āśva 13, 9.
22. Āśva, Chap. 16-19
23. Āśva, Chap. 20 to 31
24. Śānti, Chap. 139
25. Ibid., Chap. 38
26. Ibid., Chap 141.
27. Ibid., Chap 143.
28. Vaidya, C. V., The Mahābhārata, A Criticism. p. 53

1

The Notion of Dharma

The concept of Dharma plays a vital rote in the Hindu ethics. It serves as the centre of all ethical elements in the epic. In this chapter, Dharma is discussed in four parts.

I

Literally, the word 'Dharma' means 'that which holds together.' It comes from the root 'dhṛ' i.e. to hold or uphold. It signifies the basis of moral and social orders. All human beings are held together by Dharma.

The notion of Dharma is supposed to have its root in the Ṛgvedic concept of 'Ṛta'. It is analysed by D.P. Vora thus, 'Ṛta is the high order of the universe and of sacrifice. It also means ethical conduct, the true ways as opposed to its negative 'Anṛta'. It is an order instituted by the wise spirit as the regulator of the world".[1] According to prof. N. Venkataraman, Ṛta stands for the fundamental truth, harmony, unity in diversity, system or eternal moral order of the entire universe.[2] In this connection, I. C. Sharma states, "The concept of Rita has great ethico-meta physical significance. It represents the sublime moral order, which is inviolable. The inviolability of Rita makes it superior to gods and cosmic ethics on the one hand, and individual human beings on the other, because Rita works throughout the cosmos inevitably and justly. This fact implies that even in the case of an individual's action Rita, the eternal law, is responsible for the apportionment of reward and punishment."[3] According to A. B. Keith, Ṛta, in the Vedas, is a cosmic force and even the gods are subject to its laws. Ṛta means the physical order of the universe, the due order of sacrifice and the moral law in the world.[4] Here Ṛta is understood in a wider sense. It is treated as a principle, a law, a guide of the universe. The entire world is supposed not only to be based on, but also governed by 'Ṛtam' or Dharma. Hence, the ultimate nature of the universe and also the basis of human conduct are considered to depend upon Dharma which is an eternal law or perpetual order.

According to Dr. B. G. Gokhale, Ṛta, however, does not entirely disappear for it is transformed into the concept of Dharma which holds such decisive away over Indian thinking through the ages. Alongside of Ṛta the idea of Dharma also evolves in the Vedic literature. Dharma then comes to mean custom (Ṛgveda, III, 17, 1, 10), moral laws (VII, 89, 5, 11), laws of duties in general (X, 56, 3, 12), what is right (VIII, 98, 1) etc.[5] To Dr. Radhakrishnan, "In the Vedas, it is used to denote religious rites."[6] In the Brāhmaṇas, according to Keith, the concept of Dharma largely supersedes the old concept of Ṛta for obvious reasons. As the complexity of social organization increases the old concept of Ṛta is found to be inadequate where as the concept of Dharma is able to answer practically all the needs of the evolving situation.[7] According to Dr. Radhakrishnan, Dharma, then, emerges as a code of duties towards gods, seers, manes, men and the lower orders of creation.[8] According to him, "The Chāndogya Upaniṣad speaks of the three branches of Dharma, relating to the duties of the householder, the hermit and the student (Trayo Dharma Skandhā-II 23). When the Taittiriya Upaniṣad asks us to practise Dharma, (Dharmaṁ cara-1.11) it refers to the duties of the stage of life to which we belong."[9] According to P. V. Kane, "The Bṛhadāraṇyaka Upaniṣad remarks that truth and dharma are, in practical life, identical terms. One of the noblest prayers in all literatures occurs in the Bṛhadāraṇyaka Upaniṣad (1. 3.28) "From falsehood lead me unto truth, from darkness lead me unto light, from death lead me unto immortality."[10]

The Dharmasūtras present a fully developed concept of Dharma. Dharma, in these Sūtras, comes to signify a whole code of conduct to maintain the prevalent order. It includes the privileges, duties and obligations of a man, his standard of conduct as a member of the Aryan community, as a member of one of the varṇas, as a person in a particular stage of life.[11] In the Dharmasūtras, Dharma appears to U. N. Ghoshal as the sum total of the distinctive duties of the constituent units of the social system comprising the four castes (varṇas) and the four orders (āśramas).[12] In the Smṛtis when it is found with reference to the varṇas and āśramas, it clearly conveys the duties of the four varṇas - Brāhmiṇa, Kṣatriya, Vaiśya and Śūdra and āśramas - Brahmcarya, Gārhasthya, Vānaprasthya and Saṃnyāsa. E. W. Hopkins in relation to Smṛti treats Dharma as a comprehensive code of conduct. To him, it implies, "all recognized virtuous conduct, which includes in its social aspects approved usage in the matter of family-customs, caste-distinction, the stages of life to be passed through by all Aryans; in short the maintenance of established order.[13] Dharma is supposed to contain in itself the activities which shape and sustain human life. The purpose of Dharma seems to bring into an organic whole the growing and changing sentiments, interests and needs of the individual in course of time.

It would be better to refer to some of the views regarding Dharma of the early classical systems of Indian philosophy. Buddhistic thinkers consider Dharma as an empirical and subjective category. It is a vāsana or trend or disposition of the citta or mental continuum - a continuum which is annulled in the transcendental state. Dharma is only empirically significant and is subjective or mental in essence. It is an enduring trait or tendency of the mind.[14] As Dr. P. T, Raju says, Dharma in Buddhistic philosophy means a law of nature; but it also means a social law, the Varnāśramadharma or the rule of caste and Āśrama; the moral law or the ought, for example the Dharma of Ahiṁsā or non-violence; good acts like charity etc.; the nature of things as in the words like Manodharma or the nature of mind and Vastudharma or the nature of things.[15] So, it is not a natural law alone but also a social and moral law.

Kaṇāda in his Vaiśeṣika Sūtra defines Dharma as that which gives prosperity in this life (Abhyudaya) and the highest success hereafter (Niḥ-śreyasa).[16] For the Nyāya Vaiśeṣikas, righteousness and unrighteousness are the qualities of the Atman or self i.e., the subjective categories.[17] In the transcendental life, the self is free from righteousness and unrighteousness, but in the empirical life, the self becomes implicated in the moral order by righteousness and unrighteousness which are not permanent modifications of the self and can be removed by a process of spiritual discipline. The self may recover its transcendental purity.

For Sāṁkhya, it is mere function (Vṛtti) of the minds[18] since righteousness and unrighteousness do not touch the individual (Puruṣa) in his transcendental nature. They appertain only to the mind which is the modalisation of Prakṛti in the empirical state of transformation. Morality and immorality, righteousness and unrighteousness have thus only an empirical significance. They are, therefore, the functions of the mind (Manas) which is the organ of empirical life rather than attributes of the transcendental self, Atman, or Puruṣa.[19]

In the Mīmāṁsā literature, the word, 'Dharma' denotes the injunctions of the Vedas (codanā lakṣano 'rtho dharmaḥ).[20] Whatever is enjoined in the Vedavākya as a command is said to constitute a Dharma.

Śaṁkara explains the meaning of the words 'Ṛta' and 'satya' in his own way. He states 'satyam yathāśās trartdhatā sa eva anuṣṭhiyamānaḥ dharmanāmā bhavati i.e. Satya is the true import of the Śāstras and when that is translated into action, it becomes Dharma.[21]

It will not be out of place to consider here the views of some western thinkers in relation to Dharma. In the Encyclopedia of Religion and Ethics, Dharma is treated as a sacred law, duty, justice and religions, merit. It says, "Indian commentators have explained it as denoting an act which produces the quality of the soul called Apurva, the cause of heavenly bliss and of final liberation. In ordinary usage, however, it has a far wider meaning than this, and denotes established practice or custom of any caste or community."[22] John Mackenzie, in course of his comments on Dharma, points out that Dharma cannot be translated as religion, virtue, law and duty. He finds no distinction between a moral and religious duty, usage, customary observance, law and Dharma. According to him, Dharma is the term which is applied to the whole complex froms of conduct that are settled or established.[23] Charles Drekmier considers Dharma fundamental for religion.[24] He also regards Dharma as external law as well as moral law.[25] The whole saying of Dr. Drekmier may be summed up in his own words, "In short, Dharma stands for a manner of life, the whole duty of man in relation to moral, material and intellectual purpose of life."[26] To P. younger and S.O Younger, Dharma is the order which gives structure and purpose to the universe. The cosmos, society and the individual are all guided, by the principle of dharma.[27]

Heinrich Zimmer states, "Dharma is the doctrine of the duties and rights of each in the ideal society, and as such the law or mirror of all moral action."[28]

The concept of Dharma has also been elucidated by such modern Indian thinkers as Radhakumud Mookerji, H. D. Bhattacharyya, P. S. Sivaswami Aiyer, P. V. Kane, Dr. Bhagvan

Das and others. Radhakumud Mookerji takes Dharma in many senses. At one place, he accepts it as that which holds in the midst of change.[29] He equates Dharma with ceremonial religion[30] and also with Karma.[31] P. S. Sivaswami Aiyer interpretes Dharma in a still wider sense. According to him, "It is used in the senses of nature, law, justice, virtue, merit, duty and morality."[32] He further observes, "It includes what may be called self-regarding duties to deceased ancestors as well as duties to living beings."[33] Prof. H. D. Bhattacharyya asserts that Dharma is not what is prescribed by the scriptures but is the ideal in conduct, towards which we must move in order to prefect ourselves spiritually, especially as social units.[34] For him, it is the moral law as well as the law of our being from which we can not deviate, if so, only at the risk of peril. By our daily confect we build a moral destiny for ourselves and our survival and succeeding embodiments are fully determined by it. What we know or feel would not matter at the end, but how we act would determine our destiny. Dharma judges at the end, saves us if we have followed the path of rectitude (dharmo rakṣati dhārmikaṁ).[35] According to Dr. B. G. Gokhale, it (Dharma) gives meaning to human endeavour and in its all-pervasive spirit, it regulates all forms of human activity whether social or individual, moral or metaphysical, rational or mystical, mundane or spiritual.[36]

It will be significant to quote here the exhaustive interpretation of Dharma given by Pandurang Vaman Kane. By Dharma, he does not understand creed or religion but a mode of life or a code of conduct, which regulates a man's work and activities as a member of society and as an individual and is intended to bring about the gradual development of a man to enable him to reach what is deemed to be the goal of human existence.[37]

The interpretation of Dharma by Dr. Bhagvan Das is also significant. He describes Dharma thus, "The words religion, law, legal obligation are derived from Latin roots having meanings, ligare, legere, lex, legis. That which holds a thing together, makes it what it is, prevents it from breaking up and changing it into something else, its characteristic function, its peculiar property, its fundamental attribute, its essential nature, is its Dharma, the law of its being, primarily. That which makes the world-process what it is, and holds all its parts together as one whole in breakless all-binding chain of changes--and-effects, is the law (or totality of laws) of Nature or Nature's God, Dharma in the largest sense, the world-order. That scheme or code of laws which binds together human beings in the bonds or mutual rights-and-duties, of causes-and-consequences of actions, arising out of their temperamental characters, in relation to each other, and thus maintains society, is human law, Manavadharma. Yet again, "the code of life, based on Veda (all science of the laws of nature in all her departments), the due observance of which leads to happiness here and also here-after, is Dharma."[38] Citing Vaiśeṣika Sūtra Dr. Das summarises the characteristics of Dharma as follows, "Briefly Dharma is a characteristic property, scientifically; duty, morally and legally; religion with all its proper implications, psycho-physically and spiritually; and righteousness and law generally, but duty above all."[39]

Coming now to the Mahābhārata, we find that Dharma is used in almost all the shades of meaning which we have noticed above. The main characteristics of Dharma may be enumerated as follows:

(a) Dharma is a code of conduct.

(b) It holds people together.

(c) It integrates individual's character.

(d) It organises society and assures political stability.

(e) It is the performance of the Vedic rituals.

(f) it is the observance of the Dharmaśāstras.

(g) It is the following of the unconventional behaviour of the pious and learned men.

(h) It leads to worldly benefit.

(i) And finally it leads to spiritual welfare at the individual.

To sum up, Dharma in the epic stands for the code of conduct which holds people together for integrating individual's character, organising society and assuring political stability by performing Vedic rituals, observing duties of the Dharmaśāstras and following the paths trodden by the great-men leading to worldly good and spiritual welfare of the individual.

Let us elaborate with illustrations the points mentioned above in the light of the Mahābhārata.

When we say that Dharma is a code of conduct, it refers to the fact that it is a collection or group of laws or rules to judge actions as right or wrong. It directs us to perform such actions as are morally right. If anything is done not in accordance with this norm then it is regarded as wrong, otherwise it is right. If it says that non-injury is right, then whatever is done for the sake of protection, (i.e., non-injury of beings) is right and its opposite is wrong. In the Karṇaparva, there is a direct fight between Karṇa and Arjuna. Kama gets down from his chariot to raise its wheel which had sunk into the ground and Arjuna is on the point to kill him. Karṇa then says to Arjuna that it is not yudhhadharma to attack him as he (Karṇa) is unarmed.[40] But at that moment Kṛṣṇa himself justifies the action by reminding the shameful and cruel acts of denuding Draupadī and of killing Abhimanyu by a number of persons and asks him, 'Kvate dharmastadā gataḥ'[41], i.e., where had then your dharma gone? Here the word 'Dharma' clearly stands for the law or rule or code of conduct. It suggests a code of conduct for the warriors. One who violates this rule will be regarded as a wrong-doer. Thus we find that in this context, the word Dharma has been used to denote moral law.

The epic enjoins, 'Dharma dhārayati prajāḥ', i.e., Dharma holds people together.[42] In other words, to be Dharma, it must always work for sustaining and upholding people. It appears to be the binding force of the mankind. In its absence, humanity will be like the planetary system without its binding force of law of gravitation. This characteristic of Dharma is also mentioned by Dr. Sukathankar.[43] He finds it as the simplest and at the same time the most profound exposition of the subject. In the Rāmāyaṇa also, this characteristic of Dharma is emphasised. In the Prakṣipta-Sarga of the Uttarakāṇḍa, the dog compares Dharma with a king and states that it is Dharma or virtue that upholds all mankind. It is by Dharma or virtue that the three worlds are being preserved.[44]

Dharma must integrate individual's character. According to the epic, a man must always engage himself in the good and welfare of all creatures in thought, speech and deeds. He must treat all things, and all creatures equally. He must be the friend of them all. The dialogue between Jājali and Tulādhāra about Dharma throws ample light on it. Tulādhāra says to Jālali that the mode of living which is found in a total harmlessness towards all creatures or in a minimum of such harm, is the highest Dharma.[45] He further states, "O Jājali, he alone is said to know what morality or righteousness is, who is always the friend of all creatures and who is always engaged in the benefits of all in thought, speech and action. I never solicit any one, I never quarrel with any one, I never cherish aversion for anyone. I never cherish desires for anything. I cast equal eyes upon all creatures. Behold O Jājali, with respect to all treat creatures. I neither praise not blame the acts of others, viewing this variety in the world, O foremost of Brāhmiṇs, to be like the variety observable in the sky"[46]

Dharma helps in organising society. If Dharma is destroyed, the whole social system will be paralysed and there will be utter chaos and confusion. It is Dharma which determines the respective duties of the individuals. Varnāśramadhrmas point out the duties of the individuals in relation to their social status and their stage in life. Without Dharma, nobody will attach importance to his duty. The peace, progress and stability will disappear from society and no proper, just and righteous work will be performed. Only with the help of Dharma, the rulers rule their countries. Political stability will be an impossibility without it. Anarchy will prevail. Barbarism will rule society and state. One will not recognise the other. One man may be robbed by two others and many more may robe the two.[47] So Dharma controls all these factors. The rulers use their daṇḍa only in accordance with Dharma.[48]

Vedic Dharma consists mainly in the performances of rituals and sacrifices. We find traces of performances of Rājasuya yajña, Aśvamedha yajña, and Śrāddha etc. in the Mahāhhārata. The epic recognises the performances of these sacrifices as Dharma.[49] Dharma as observance of Vedic injunctions is maintained at many places in the Mahābhārata. In the Vanaparva, the 'Dharma Vyādha' (virtuous butcher) says to the Brāhmiṇ Kauṣika that what is said in the Vedas is Dharma.[50] Here we find 'Dharma' used in the Mīmāṁsā sense.

Observance of duties assigned by Dharmaśāstras is also regarded as Dharma. The duties pertaining to the four varṇas and the four stages are highly regarded. They are known as Varnāśramadharmas. In the Bhagavadgītā, when Kṛṣṇa is advising Arjuna to fight having regard to what his Dharma is, he points out the duties of his varṇa 'svadharmapi cāvekṣya.'[51] Further when he says that it is better to die performing Sva-dharma: and to follow Para-dharma is dangerous,[52] he hints towards the duties of the four varṇas. Observance of Sanātanadharma is also recognized in the epic. The Mahābhārata, quoting Manu says-"The practices of abstention from injury, truthfulness of speech, justice, compassion, self-restraint, procreation upon one's wives amiability, modesty, patience are the best Dharma.[53] There are separate duties mentioned for each order but there are certain duties which must be performed by all the four orders. They are called Sāmanyadharma and also Sanātanadharma. Bhīśma states, "The suppression of wrath, truthfulness of speech, justice, forgiveness, begetting children upon one's wedded wives, purity of conduct, avoidance of quarrel, simplicity, the maintenance of dependents, these nine duties belong to all the four orders equally."[54] There are other duties too like Rājadharma, the duty of king, Prajādharma- the duty of subjects, Kuladharma, the duty pertaining to class of family, etc.

To follow the unconventional behaviour of great-men is also considered as a Dharma. In the Vanaparva, Yudhiṣṭhira is asked by Yakṣa as to which is the path of Dharma. Yudhiṣṭhira replies: Mahājano yena gataḥ sapanthāḥ' i.e., the path which has been followed by venerable or great persons is the path of Dharma.[55] Dharma is sometimes considered to have originated from the rules laid by reverend people and it be acceptable to all as respectable behaviour or Śiṣṭacāra. In the Mahābhārata and also in the Smṛtis, these are such statements as "ācāraprabhavo dharmaḥ'.[56] Maheśvara states in the Anuśāsanaparva that Dharma follows from the Vedas, Smṛtis and Śiṣṭācārā or behaviour laid down by great reverend men'[57] The same is stated in the Vanaparva also.[58] Vyāsa says to Yudhiṣṭhira that to get pleasure in this world and in the other, man must follow the path paved by great men.[59]

Dharma leads to Abhyudaya, i.e., worldy prosperity of the individual who performs it. Through Dharma, he gets wealth (Artha) and he secures happiness in life. His desires are satisfied. Vyāsa himself observes in the Bhārata Sāvitrī,:-

"O people I am haranguing you with raised hands, no one listens to me. If both wealth (Artha) and desires (Kāma) can be acquired by Dharma, why not follow such a Dharma."[60] As in the Vaiśeṣka--sūtra, so in the Mahābhārata also, Dharma is hoped to give earthly benefits to the individual and it also leads the individual to final liberation for which each and every individual aspires. Bhīṣma states in this connection, "what is done for the prosperity and welfare of the beings is Dharma."[61] Kṛṣṇa also states in the Karṇaparva that Dharma is preached for both Abhyudaya and Niḥśreyasa of the individuals.[62] On another occasion, Bhīṣma observes, "In both the worlds, that is, here and hereafter Dharma produces happiness.[63] Kapila states that benevolence, forgiveness, tranquillity, compassion, truthfulness and candour, abstention from injury, absence of pride, modesty, renunciation and abstention from work are the paths that lead to Brahman. By those, one attains to what is the Highest.[64] So it is Dharma by which one can attain his supreme goal. Hence Dharma leads to spiritual benefit which is the final end of all.

It may be relevant here to mention what modern scholars say about Dharma as enunciated in the Mahābhārata. Chintamani Rao Vaidya writes that the Mahābhārata teaches us to adhere to Dharma in all situations howsoever difficult they may be. By Dharma, he means all the duties of man towards God and his ownself.[65] Dr. T.M.P. Mahadevan means by Dharma, good or righteousness, duty and religious merit, which are related senses, each with an ethical significance. It is out of the goodness of an individual that a willing devotion to his duty proceeds; and as a result of conscientious performance of his allotted work, a person reaps merit, though he may not consciously aim at it. And, it is through Dharma, again, that he goes beyond the relativities of life and thus gains freedom from bondage.[66] Swami Siddhenathananda takes Dharma as good conduct which conduces to liberation and also as the support of the world.[67] Dr. B. L. Atreya interprets Dharma as a law which governs our activities so that all beings in the universe may live peacefully with one another and may be happy, may get wealth according to their necessity and may also get pleasure of both of this world and of the other (heaven).[68]

In summing up, we find that it (Dharma) is an ethical principle because it prescribes 'ought' for us. It suggests as to what our moral action should be. It judges our action as good or bad and right or wrong. It is a code of social conduct as it points out what should be our social duties and obligations to preserve the social unity and social stability for both individual and social good. Social welfare is not at all possible when there is confusion in society. It is due to Dharma alone that man progresses in society and attains his final goal of Brahma-Realisation. It is a political code as it helps Kings or rulers in ruling their countries. Without Dharma, the political principle, a kingdom cannot be maintained. It is a check on both kings and their subjects. It determines the function of the king and the people. Without the king, there will be anarchy in the kingdom and all work will remain paralysed. So, Dharma is essential for statecraft. It is also binding on the people prescribed by the ancient seers and saints for respective vocations. It is also supposed to be the spiritual binding force which sustains the universe. Hence, it may also be regarded as a spiritual principle. Thus we can conclude that Dharma in the epic is an ethico-socio-politico-spiritual principle.

II

Broadly speaking, Dharma may be subsumed under two heads - (i) Sāmānya or general and (ii) Viśeṣa or specific. The former are usually meant for all; the latter are meant for particular Varṇas, specific stations in life and special circumstances. Sāmānya or Sādhāraṇa Dharmas include:-

1. Ahiṁsā - Harmlessness,
2. Satya - Truthfulness,
3. Akrodha - Non-anger,
4. Tapa - Austerity,
5. Kṣamā - Forgiveness ,
6. Dāna - gift ,
7. Dama - Control of sense-organs,
8. Dayā - Compassion,
9. Anirṣyā - Non-enmity,
10. Amātsarya - Absence of pride,
11. Aṇasuyā-Not to find faults with others,
12. Śīla - Good manners,
13. Ārjava-Simplicity,
14. Samvibhāga - Distribution of wealth,
15. Hṛ-(lajja)- Modesty,
16. Titikṣā - Tolerance of mind.'
17. Śama - Tranquillity of mind,
18. Śānti - peace,
19. Alobha - Freedom from greed,
20. prajanah svasudārecṣu-To give birth to children from one's own wife,
21. Asteya-Non stealing.

All the Dharmas mentioned above are not enumerated at one place in the great epic but can be collected from different contexts. In the Vanaparva, only eight Dharmas have been innmerated.[69] But in the Śāntiparva, Bhīṣma enlists ten Dharmas[70] at one place and nine at another.[71] In yet another context, sevenfold Dharmas have been regarded as seven gates of heaven.[72]

It is worth mentioning here that the emphasis has not been laid equally on all Dharmas simultaneously. It appears that due stress has been laid on Dharmas in accordance with the contexts. For this simple reason, Dharmas are mentioned in different numbers varying from seven to ten at a time. It may be held that if all Dharmas are given equal treatment simultaneously, it may be difficult for an individual to practise all Dharmas at a time since Dharmas may conflict with one another in varying circumstances.

We can compare this account with a list of Sādhāraṇa Dharma in the Rāmāyaṇa. They are - gift of food,[73] all gifts with due honour,[74] show of respect to guests,[75] forgiveness and forbearance,[76] modesty and self-control,[77] softness leading to contempt,[78] check to wrong doing even by the great,[79] giving and heeding good counsel,[80] sweetness,[81] loyalty to comrades,[82] help to friends,[83] truth,[84] help to the good - end succour to the hurt,[85] requital of help and gratitude,[86] chivalry and reverence to womanhood,[87] purity of mind,[88] prayer for long life,[89] good conduct,[90] equanimity,[91] simultaneous skill,[92] desisting from causing harms.[93]

Vyāsa asks one of the aspirants, "Do as you would be done by. Do unto others, as you wish others to do unto you. You will be saved from all troubles. If you follow these wise maxims you can never give any pain unto others. Practise this in your daily life."[94] In the Śāntiparva, Bhīṣma also asserts it while describing the nature of Dharma.[95] Here it is pointed out that a man should not behave in the manner which he himself dislikes to receive in his turn. We generally expect that nobody should cause harm to us either physically or mentally. We also expect that none should behave untruthfu-lly to us. Keeping these things in mind, we should also adopt harmlessness and truthfulness towards others. For this reason alone, harmlessness and truthfulness are regarded as most important Dharmas. In the Ādiparva, it is observed, "Ahiṁsā parmodharmaḥ.[96] Hīṁsā does not only mean to destroy life but it also means to harm even the mind. It is looked upon as the highest Dharma. In the Śāntiparva, Bhīṣma maintains that no body should be harmed. For this reason, Dharma is preached. Hence harmlessness is Dharma.[97] The superiority of harmlessness is repeatedly mentioned in the Mahābhārata. Again in the Śāntiparva, Tulādhāra says to Jājali that no Dharma is superior to the Dharma which maintains harmlessness or non-injury of beings.[98] "To follow 'Ahiṁsā' or harmlessness is the best method of the welfare of men," is stated by Bṛhaspati to Yudhiṣṭhira in the Anuśāsanaparva.[99] Again in the same prava, the superiority of Ahiṁsā is repeatedly maintained.[100] Bhīṣma also says to Yudhiṣṭhira, "Persons conversant with Dharma (duty) say, that Dharma is worthy of being called Dharma which has abstention from cruelty for its indication. The man of cleansed soul should do only such acts as have compassion for their soul.[101] Further he observes that Ahiṁsā or Harmlessness is the supreme Dharma, it is the supreme restraint, supreme gift, and supreme austerity. It is **the supreme sacrifice (yañja), it is the supreme result, it is the** supreme fruit and it is the supreme pleasure.[102]

The next important Dharma is Satya or truthfulness. Truth is accepted by all men and by all religions of the world. The value of Satya is rightly described at many places in the Mahābhārata, "Nāstī Satyāt paro dharma" i.e., there is no Dharma higher than truth.[103] Again in the Śāntiparva, Bhīṣma states that where there is truth, there is always Dharma. Truth is ancient Dharma, truth alone should be worshipped; truth, indeed, is the very supreme. Truth is virtue, austerity and yoga; truth is the ageless Brahman, truth is said to be the supreme sacrifice, in truth is everything established.[104]

In the Anuśāsanaparva, Maheśvara defines 'satya' as that which is expressed by speech without any change as it has been seen and done.[105] In the Ādīparva, Śakuntalā states to Duṣyanta the merit of truth that when the respective merits of a thousand aśvamedha yajñas and truth are weighed in the scale, it is found that truth weighed more heavily.[106] There are many other verses in the Ādiparva which indicate the superiority of truthfulness over other Dharmas.[107] Bhīṣma's last teachings to Yudhiṣṭhira is that truth is the sum and substance of all Dharmas. He states, 'satyeṣu yatitavyaṁ vaḥ satyam hi param balam" i.e., that you should strive for truth, in as much as truth is the highest power.[108]

Kṣamā or forgiveness is regarded as an important Dharma. Yudhiṣṭhira states to Draupadī in the Vanaparva that those persons whose anger is overpowered by forgiveness attain the higher regions, therefore forgiveness is considered as one of the highest virtues.[109] Further he observes that forgiveness and humanity are the eternal Dharmas.[110] Again in the same chapter, forgiveness is identified with yajña, Veda, Śāstra, truthfulness, austerity and even with the Brahman. And the entire, world is supposed to depend on it.[111]

Asteya or non-stealing is an important Dharma. Control of the sense-organs is also placed on the same level with Ahiṁṣā and Satya. Desires (Kāmā), Anger (Krodha) and Avarice (lobha) are regarded as enemical to man. Without bringing them under full control, neither man nor society will be, in any way, benefited. It is observed both in the Viduranīti and in the Bhagavadgītā that Kāma, Krodha and Lobha are the three gateways to hell; and as they are destructive agent, they must be eschewed.[112] In the Anuśānaparva, Maheśvara says to his wife Umā that one who controls his sense-organs is wise and happy. By controlling senses and offering gifts, man attains everything which he wishes.[113] Bhīṣma states that controlling of the senses is superior to gift. A generous man may be angry at the time of offering- gift but sense-controlled man cannot be so. Hence, controlling of senses is regarded as superior to gift.[114] That self-control is supreme is also found at other places. He stresses his contention by treating self-control as unique since it is the sum total of all these dharmas.[115] It is also regarded as the highest of virtues in the world and a person can acquire the highest happiness both here and hereafter through it.[116]

Non-accumulation is one of the most important Dharmas mentioned in the epic. In the Śāntiparva, Yudhiṣṭhira explains to Arjuna the utility of wealth that it is for sacrifice and gift but not for accumulation. He states that wealth has been created for the sake of sacrifices and all wealth should be applied to sacrifices. It is not proper to spend wealth for the gratification of desires of enjoyment. One should spend (in gift) what one has acquired and not waste and spend in satisfying one's desires.[117] He further states, "These are the two faults connected with wealth even when acquired, viz., gift to an undeserving person and abstaining from giving unto him that is deserving."[118]

Non-anger is one of the significant Dharmas, mentioned in the epic. Krodha (anger) is considered as one of the inborn vices of human nature along with Kāma and Lobha. The conquest of anger leads to control of the senses. Kṛṣṇa describes anger as the cause of destruction in the Gītā. He thus, says 'from anger arises bewilderment, from bewilderment, loss of memory; and from loss of memory, the destruction of intelligence and from the destruction of intelligence, he perishes.[119] In the epic Sanatsujāta in enumerating the elemental twelve vices in a person, places anger at the head of the list.[120] In the Ādiparva, Śukra advises his daughter Devayānī to subdue her anger pointing out the evil consequences of it. He states that one who does not mind the evil speeches of others conquers every thing. A man is regarded as man if he practises forgiveness shaking off his rising anger like snake casting off its slough. He who suppresses his anger and does not mind the evil speeches of others by not becoming angry, certainly acquires virtue, wealth, desire and salvation.[121]

Other Dharmas are also given due importance in the Mahābhārata. It may be mentioned here in this connection that none of them should be ignored and neglected. Every one of them should be adopted in life. These Dharmas which we discussed earlier are meant for all, restive of class, stage, sex and age.

Dharma are supposed to be divided in many ways, although no systematic account of all subdivisions seems possible. Specific Dharmas are divided in many ways. According to S. V. Ketkar, one of the ways of subdividing Dharma is: (1) Dharma for individual (purṣa-dharma or vyakti-dharma), (2) Dharma respecting family - kula-dharma, (3) Dharma respecting the tribe or caste (jati-dharma) and (4) Dharma respecting the nation or the country (Deśadharma or Raṣṭra-Dharma).[122] The classification is based on the birth of the individual. When there is a clash between these Dharmas or in other words, when the duties of one group clash with the duties of another, the interest of the smaller group should be sacrificed to the larger. For example, it is mentioned in the Ādiparva, "For the sake of the family individual should be abandoned, for the sake of village even the family should be abandoned, and for the sake of the country the village be abandoned,[123]"

Sometimes Dharma is also classified on the basis of sex. Dharma of a man (Puruṣa-dharma) is really different from that of the woman (Strī-dharma). For example: in the epic, the she-pigeon observes the duties of a woman that she is no wife with whom her lord is not content. In the case of women, if their lords be gratified with them all the duties also become so.[124] It is further observed that wife with whom her husband is not pleased becomes consumed into ashes, even like a creeper adorned with bunches of flowers in a forest conflagration.[125]

In this connection, the division maintained by P. V. Kane should be considered here. According to him, Dharma is divided into Śrauta and Smārta. The first comprises those rites and ceremonies with which the Vedic Saṁhitās and Brāhmaṇas are chiefy concerned, such as consecration of the three fires, the Fullmoon and New moon sacrifices. The Smārta comprises those topics thar are specially dealt with by the Smṛtis and that concern the various classes and stages of life.[126] P. V. Kane's comprehensive classification of Dharma is six fold, i.e., (i) Dharma of Varṇas (injunctions based on varṇa alone such as a Brāhmin should never drink wine), (ii) Āśramadharma (such rules as begging and carrying a staff enjoined on a brahmcārī), (iii) Varṇāśramadharma (rules of conduct enjoined on a man because he belongs to a particular class and is in a particular stage of life such as a Brāhmin-Brahmacāri should carry a staff of Palāsa tree), (iv) Guṇadharma (such as protection of subjects is the case of a crowned king), (v) Naimittikadharma (such as expiation on doing what is forbidden), (vi) Sādhāraṇadharma (what is common to all humanity viv., Ahiṁsā and other virtues)[127].

Like Kane's first classification in the great epic, we find that there are Dharmas classified as Śrauta and Smārta but in it, there is one more Dharma named as Śiṣṭācāra. In the Anuśāsanaparva as well as in the Vanaparva, it is mentioned that there are three Dharmas. The first is what is enjoined by the Vedas, the second Dharma is what is prescribed in the Dharmśāstra and the third is Śiśtācāra.[128]

Dharma is also divided on the basis of varṇa and āśrama of the individual in the epic. An individual's Dharmas are determined according to the class or varṇa, to which he belongs. On the basis of class, Dharmas are divided into four-Brāhmaṇa

Dharma, Kṣātra Dharma, Vaiśya Dharma and Śūdra Dharma. For example, Bhīṣma in the first lesson to Yudhiṣṭhira about the duties of a Brāhmin, states that by his study of the Vedas all the pious acts (laid down for the Brāhmiṇ) are accomplished. Whether he does or does not achieve anything else, if he devotes himself to the study of the Vedas, he becomes (by that) known as a Brāhmin or the friend of all creatures.[129] There is one more Dharma belonging to Varṇasaṁkaras who are outside this fourfold scheme of Varṇa-Dharma. They have their own Dharmas. For example, Dharmas of the Varṇasaṁkara are determined by his father and mother. In the Anuśānaparva, Bhīṣma maintains that the son begotten through transgression, by a Śūdra upon a Kṣatrīya woman, becomes a Niṣāda and the duties assigned to him have reference to the catching of fish. If a Śūdra happens to have intercourse with a Vaisya woman, the son begotten upon her comes to be called Ayngava, The duties assigned to such a person are that of a Takṣan (Carpenter).[130] Throughout the epic, we find descriptions of different Dharmas for the different classes for the benefits of each class.

Dharma is further classified in accordance with the āśrama or the stage of life of the individual. Corresponding to four stages, there are four-fold Dharmas, viz., Dharmas of (1) Brahmacaryāśrama, (2) Gṛhasthāśrama, (3) Vanaprasthāśrama and (4) Saṁnyāśarama. Dharma of an individual is determined by the āśrama or station of life to which he belongs at a particular time. For example, a Saṁnyāsin must have control over his mind and senses and must lead a life of an ascetic without having any desire.[131]

Besides Varṇāśramadharmas, there is one more kind of Dharma in the epic which is called 'Āpaddarma'. It is a Dharma of emergency. In times of distress, one is allowed to follow these Dharmas. For example, to read and teach the Vedas and to perform and help others in performing yajñas are the normal duties of the Brāhmin. But it is also observed in the epic by Bhīṣma that at the time of distress a Brāhmin can adopt the duties of Kaṣtriya and even of Vaiśya.[132]

In the epic, we trace one more Dharma named Guṇadharma. Guṇadharma follows from the very nature of the thing. Yugadharma follows from the very name of a particular age. Yugadharmas follow according to the prevalent age.[133]

III

Whether Dharma is absolute or relative in the epic is an important question to be discussed. If Dharma is to be absolute, it must remain the same at all places, in all the circumstances and for all the persons. In other words, absolute Dharma is that Dharma which is maintained in all the cases irrespective of circumstances and situations. Relative Dharma is that Dharma which varies according to change in time and place. In the great epic, we find that Dharma is relative and not absolute. It is a fact that Dharma is given a very high status in the epic. There are Dharmas corresponding to war- time and also to peace-time. Some of them correspond to abnormal times or crises. Yudhiṣṭhira declares in the Śāntiparva that the duties of a person who is well off, are of one kind and those of a person who has fallen into distress are of another kind.[134] We do not find any Dharma in the epic which remains the same, irrespective of different situations, place and time.

There is a tendency in Indian thinkers to postulate an absolute and high ideal of Dharma. That ideal is known as 'Mahāvrata. Patanjali propoundes this ideal in his Yogasūtra as, above space and time. In the Yogasūtra it is observed, "Jātideśakāla samayanava cchināḥ sarvabhaumāḥ Mahāvrataḥ,"[135] i.e., the Mahāvrata is that which is universal, unconditioned by the nature of thing, place and circumstances. Patanjali brings five Dharmas namely - Ahiṁsā, Satya, Asteya, Brahmcarya and Aparigraha under this higher ideal of Mahāvrata.[136] Even these Dharmas which are regarded as universal and above time and space by Patanjali are not quite absolute. They also are relative to circumstances. We can cite a number of examples from the Mahābhārata to show that in the case of a conflict between two such Dharmas, one has got to be abandoned for the sake of the other. In our day to day life too there takes place a conflict between Ahiṁsā and Satya, between the benefit of the individual himself and the benefit of others. This sort of moral conflict does arise not only in the ordinary people's mind but also in the life of greatmen like Arjuna, Yudhiṣṭhira and other important characters of the epic. Preaching Ahiṁsā, Kṛṣṇa inspires Arjuna to enter into the fierce war of Kurukṣetra. Arjuna is not in favour of such war and he thinks to discard it for the sake of precious lives of his relatives and preceptors. He is even ready to live on alms than to kill his people and enjoy the kingdom of Hastinapura.[137] Yudhiṣṭhira who is the symbol of truth is forced to speak a lie for an advantage in the war. Kṛṣṇa advises Yudhighira to speak a lie on the ground that if Drona fights even for half a day more, then the whole army of Yudhiṣṭhira would be destroyed.[138] And he does so for protecting the army and winning the battle. Thus in the epic, we get divergent ways in which these Dharmas are preached and practised.

We will now explain these Dharmas - general and particular with illustrations from the epic whether they are absolute or relative. Let us start with Ahiṁsā or harmlessness. We notice 'Ahiṁsā parmo dharmaḥ'[139] at so many places repeatedly in the epic. But yet it is not treated as absolute. It is regarded as relative-varying from time to time and place to place. It is true that Ahiṁsā is a supreme Dharma but we are not advised by the epic to observe it in all cases. There are many occasions when we act just contrary to it and that is regarded as justified. We cannot sit idle when our life will be in danger and troubles. Ahiṁsā does not mean that one should not protect oneself when his life is in danger.

The slaughter of animals for the purpose of ritualistic sacrifices is considered just, even by the Vadas, Manusmṛtī and the Mahābhārata. Manusmṛti enjoins, "Yajñaya jagdhirmāṁsasyetyeṣa devo vidhin smṛtaḥ," i.e., for the ritualistic purpose to eat meat is preseribed.[140] In the Mahābhārata, gods state that ritual sacrifices should be performed by 'Aja' which means he-goat'[141] It is observed in the epic that Ahiṁsā cannot be fully maintained. It is an impossibility. Arjuna states that there are in the universe so many micro-organisms invisible to the naked eye, of which the existence can, however, be imagined, that merely by the moving of one's eye-lids, their limbs will be destroyed.[142] He further remarks that he sees no man who is living without killing anything because a big living being finishes the life of small beings. It is because the mongoose eats the mouse and itself is eaten by a cat and a cat in its turn is eaten by a dog and a dog by a tiger.[143] In the epic, there is a very famous story of a Brāhmin who becomes angry and attempts to curse a virtuous woman and she sends him to a butcher asking him to learn the true import of Dharma. The butcher (Dharmavyādhā) earns his livelihood by selling meat and is very much devoted to his parents. The Brāhmiṇ is much surprised to observe the way in which the virtuous butcher earns his livelihood. The butcher opens the eyes of the Brāhmin by explaining the true nature of Dharma and specially of Ahiṁsā.[144] Dharmavyādhā points out that the violence is committed in the normal life and declares, 'Ahiṁsā has been accepted as a great ideal by the people, O, best of the Brāhmiṇs, is there anybody on this earth, who does not not kill any creature? I think that there is no person... The only difference to be found is that the ascetics due to their conscious attempts, commit less violence than the others."[145]

Thus, we find in the first place that to practise Ahiṁsā in its strict sense is an extreme ideal, which cannot be practised in toto. And secondly, for the preservation of life and for the cause of peace and stability in society, Hiṁsā is permitted whenever it is necessitated. Hence harmlessness cannot be regarded as an absolute principle.

The next important Dharma is truthfulness which is regarded as a supreme Dharma in the epic. But it is also not absolute. About the relative nature of Satya or truthfulness the virtuous butcher says, "When life is at stake and in the matter of marriage it is proper to tell an untruth. Untruth sometimes leads to the triumph of truth and the latter dwindles into untruth.[146]" He further observes that wise men treat it as Dharma if it benefits the living beings when uttered. Hence Adharma is regarded as Dharma and Adharma becomes Dharma as the nature of Dharma is very subtle.[147] The relativity of Dharma is also stated by Manu in the Śāntiparva. According to him, the same action at different places and times becomes Dharma or Adharma. Adharma like stealing, speaking untruth and killing, is regarded Dharma in special circumstances.[148] Bhīṣma says that when untruth functions as truth and trust becomes untrust, in those circumstances truth should not be spoken and rather a lie should be spoken.[149] He again maintains that untruth may be spoken at the time of danger to life, at the time of marriage, for saving the wealth of others and for saving Dharma.[150] Though truth is a general Dharma, in special circumstances to speak a lie is allowed and thus, it is treated as a relative Dharma.

In the Karṇaparva, Kṛṣṇa declares that there is no sin in speaking an untruth on the following four occasions namely, in joke, at the time of marriage, or if life is in danger, and when the lives of relatives are in danger.[151] Saint Nārada says to Śuka in the Śāntiparva on the authority of Sanatkumara, "It is always proper to speak the truth. It is better again to speak what is beneficial than to speak what is true. I hold that that is truth which is fraught with the greatest benefit in all creatures."[152] Kṛṣṇa maintains five occasions when falsehood becomes truth. According to him, 'On an occasion of marriage, or of enjoying a woman or when life is in danger, or one's entire property is about to be taken away, or for the sake of a brāhmiṇ, falsehood may be sinless. On these occasions, falsehood would become truth and truth would become falsehood. He is a fool that practises truth without knowing the difference between truth and falsehood. One is said to be conversant with morality when one is able to distinguish between truth and falsehood."[153] Kṛṣṇa reveals the mystery of Dharma to Arjuna thus: "One who speaks truth is righteous. There is nothing higher than truth. Behold, however, truth as practised is exceedingly difficult to be understood as regards its essential attributes. Truth may be unutterable and even falsehood may be utterable where falsehood would become truth and truth would become falsehood.'[154] Vyāsa himself states to Yudhiṣṭhira that falsehood may be spoken for saving one's own life or that of another, or for the sake of one's preceptor, or for gratifying a women, or for bringing about a marriage.[155]

In this connection, two stories narrated by Kṛṣṇa must be explained. The first deals with a hunter, Balāka who follows unknowingly a blind beast and kills it. In return, he is bodily taken to heaven as a greater benefactor of the people from ravages; whereas the second deals with a religious Brāhmiṇ named Kauśika who because of his truthfulness reveals to the robbers where the travellers are hiding and thus gets them killed at the hands of those robbers, and in result he goes to hell.[156] Balāka while killing that blind animal has no desire to free people of the danger, nor does the Brāhmiṇ want the travellers to be killed. So it is the result of an act which decides whether the act should be regarded as Dharma or not. Here, killing the beast become Dharma and to speak truth becomes Adharma. The above view of the concept of truth reveals the fact that truth, though held as the highest ethical value for the individuals, is not to be applied in all cases. Whether a truth ought to be spoken or not depends upon place, time and circumstances. Thus Satya is also relative.

In connection with celibacy, it may be said that we are not told in the epic to practise it throughout life. If all of us decide to practise it in our life, then the entire human race will come to an end within a few decades. There will be nothing like human beings on the earth. There are so many instances in the epic which prove that even great saints, for procreating a son, have come in contact with women. Sage Ṛṣyaśṛṁga marries Śantā the daughter of King Lomapāda is stated in the Vanaparva.[157] Saint Cyavana marries Sukanyā even at such old age when he is unable to speak due to weakness.[158] According to Hindu mythology, it is a Dharma to beget son for Śrāddha and other Saṁskāras. We notice in the Ādiparva that Bhīṣma is requested to beget a son on the two wives of Vicitravirya who dies without any son.[159] Bhīṣma refuses to do so and Vyāsa comes to rescue the whole Kuru family from destruction. Thus, Pāṇḍu and Dhṛtaraṣṭra are born.[160]

The Mahābhārata regards Asteya or non-stealing as an important Dharma. We disregard a person as a sinner if he saves his life by committing theft. There is an interesting story in the epic which justifies an act of stealing. The sage Viśvāmitra, as a result of famine for 12 years, comes on the point of saving his life by stealing a dog's flesh hung up in the house of a butcher. He defends his act by saying that at the time of calamities, for saving the life, it is just and proper to steal things from the houses of high, equal and lower status of people.[161] Thus, we find that Asteya or non-stealing also is relative.

Forgiveness or Kṣamā is one of the most important Dharmas propounded in the Mahābhārata, But it too is very difficult to be practised always. In the epic, Prahlāda points out to his grandson Vali that people will not stop at openly running away with even the wife and children of man who is always peaceful. And he advises Vali that forgiveness in all cases or war likeness in all cases is not the proper thing: He thus states, "Might is not always meritorious and forgiveness also is not always meritorious."[162] He further states that "He who forgives always, O My son suffers many evils - servants, strangers and enemies always disregard him."[163]

The worship of father and mother is looked upon as an important Dharma. They are often regarded as duties, yet it is stated in the epic that because the mother of Paraśurāma commits a gracious sin, so at the instance of his father, he cuts her throat.[164]

The Mahābhārata states, "Preceptor is regarded as superior to the mother and father."[165] But it is also observed in the epic that if the preceptors are on the wrong track, they should be punished. Marutta states in this connection, 'Even a preceptor, who disregards what ought to be done and what ought not to be done and takes up arrogantly the wrong path, deserves punishment."[166] It is repeatedly mentioned at several places in the epic.

Thus, we find that the epic regards Dharmas as relative. They are so, because in human life, situations and circumstances are beyond control and an individual has to act according to changing situations. If he goes on performing the same Dharma in all places, indiscriminately, he is liable to commit many wrongs. Thus, it is clearly stated in the epic that Dharma becomes Adharma at different circumstances in different places and times.[167] It is obvious that Vyāsa is aware of the complex situations which human beings have to face in life. Hence he has elaborately discussed in several chapters the nature of Āpaddharma.[168] These Āpaddharmas are meant for times of calamities or emergent situations. They are to be followed not in normal situations of life but in abnormal circumstances, e.g., when life, and property are in danger.

In this connection, we can quote the view of Sushil Kumar De, who observes: "The theory of āpaddharma or expediency, no doubt, which lays down a practical source of conduct, not usually proper but allowable in times of extreme necessity or distress, shows that the idea of virtue and,vice was admitted to be relative and dependent on circumstances."[169]

Coming over to the Varṇāśra madharmas, we find that they are obviously relative to specific classes and stages in life, but even in their own spheres they are not absolutely binding. For example, the duties of the Brāhmiṇs are purely intellectual, such as to study and teach the Vedas, but there are occasions on which even a Brāhmiṇ is justified in taking up arms. In the Śāntiparva Bhīśma states to Yudhiṣṭhira that the Brāhmiṇ, by taking up arms, on these three occasions does not commit sin, i.e., for protecting himself, for compelling others to betake themselves to their duties and for chastising robbers.[170] Not only Brāhmiṇs, but even other classes are also permitted to take up arms, which is not their normal duty. It is observed that when robbers, breaking through all restraint, spread devastation around, all the orders may take up arms. By doing so they incur no sin.[171] It is pointed out in the epic that at the time of distress, a Brāhmiṇ can adopt the duties of a Kṣatriya and even of a Vaiśya.[172] That a Śūdra may take recourse to agriculture, cattle rearing as a means to earning livelihood, is observed in the Parāśaragītā.[173]

At the very outset, we have mentioned that Dharma is prescribed for worldly, and spiritual development of the individual. Had Dharma been absolute, people would have been under a kind of compulsion to adopt Dharmas irrespective of time, place and situation. But it is quite clear in the Mahābhārata that an individual is at liberty to choose Dharma according to the changing needs of time, space and situations. If it is a time of normalcy, people should follow normal Varṇāśramadharma but if, unfortunately, a time of distress and calamities comes, then the individual has every right to follow an Āpaddharma or emergent duty.

In the light of these various illustrations found in the epic, it can be said that Dharma in the eyes of the epic is a relative concept. We may conclude with the sayings of Yudhiṣṭhira in the Śāntiparva, "Many great men, again turning beck (from the duties of their own order) betake themselves to the duties of the kingly order. No such conduct therefore, is to be seen (as observed by any man), which is fraught with universal benevolence. By a certain course of conduct one becomes really meritorious. That very course of conduct obstructs another in the acquisition of merit. Another, by practising at his pleasure that conduct, it is seen, remains unchanged. Thus that conduct by which one becomes meritorious impedes another in the acquisition of merit. One may thus see that all courses of conduct are seen to lose singleness of purpose and character."[174]

It is obvious now that Dharma is relative and not absolute according to the Mahābhārata.

IV

Often it is asked whether Dharma is an end in itself for human beings who adopt it in their lives. And it is also sometimes asked, whether Dharma should be not performed for the sake of any worldly gain and even for the satisfaction of desires. Our earlier study suggests that Dharma leads to prosperity and liberation of the individual. Thus Dharma is a means to these ends. But it is significant to note here that there are occasions in the epic when Dharma is maintained as an end in itself. In the Gītā Kṛṣṇa advises Arjuna to do his duties without any regard for consequences. He thus observes, "Karmaṇyevādhikārarṭe māphaleṣu kadācaṇa," i.e., your right is to work only but never to the fruit thereof. Let not the fruit of action be your object nor let your attachment be to inaction.[175] So Kṛṣṇa suggests here to perform Dharma not for any reward, but for its own sake.

On innumerable occasions, it is propounded in the epic that only Dharma is supreme and nothing else. Vidura observes in the Śāntiparva that all saints have crossed the vast sea of the universe only in and through Dharma, and the whole world depends on it for its existence. It is by virtue of Dharma that gods attain their position of superiority.[176]

It is accepted that Dharma should be followed, but the question arises, whether Dharma is to be followed for its own sake or for the sake of something else.

The character of Yudhiṣṭhira suggests that Dharma should be followed for its own sake. Yudhiṣṭhira is called Dharmarāja, i.e., he is regarded as the incarnation of Dharma. He is a part of Dharma.[177] The whole life of Yudhiṣṭhira being the son of Dharma, supports the view that Dharma is as an end in itself for him. By his word, action and thought; it is evident in the Mahābhārata that Dharma is not a means to any end. In this connection, he states to Draupadī in the Vanaparva, "I do not, O princess, follow Dharma with an eye to reward. I give simply because it is my duty to give; I sacrifice, because I must do so. Be there, any reward or not, whatever must be performed by a householder, I do it, O Draupadī, according to my ability, I practise Dharma with no regard to its fruits. I follow the scriptures and the examples of goodness. My mind is fixed upon Dharma for its own sake, O Draupadī, because it is naturally inclined to do so. He who practises Dharma for its reward traffics in Dharma and contemptible among those who talk of Dharma."[178] These lines clearly indicate the attitude of Yudhiṣṭhira towards Dharma as an end in itself. Draupadī also accepts this fact.[179] She confirms that his (Yudhiṣṭhira's) kingdom is for Dharma and even his life is for Dharma is known by Brāhmins, superiors and even celestials.[180] She believes that he (Yudhiṣṭhira) can go to any length for Dharma and she knows it well that he can leave, Bhīma, Arjuna, Nakula and Sahadeva and even her but cannot leave Dharma.[181] It is clear from the facts that Yudhiṣṭhira throughout his life, practised Dharma as an end in itself.

Dharma is treated as the summum bonum of life by Vidura also. He requests people to control the mind and to make themselves Dharma-dominated. According to him, Dharma is the first, Artha is the second and Desire is the last in point of merit. Hence one should live giving attention to Dharma.[182] Bhīṣma also maintains that Dharma is the only goal of life. For him, "they that have no reverence for virtue (Dharma) are as vile among men as seedless grains among corn or the gnat among birds."[183] To him, "The base and root of this universe is Dharma, there is nothing superior to Dharma."[184] In the Bhāṛata-Sāvitri Vyāsa himself accepts the eternity of Dharma. He concludes his saying thus, 'Never from desire, not from fear, and greed, should Dharma be renounced; so, not even for the sake of preserving life; Dharma is eternal, pleasure and pain are evanescent. The soul is eternal; the means of life are non-eternal."[185] It is also mentioned in the Udyogaparva.[186]

In the Rāmāyaṇa also, Dharma is given higher status than that of Artha and Kāma. Of them all, Dharma is supreme and the source of Artha and Kāma (legitimate enjoyment). Sītā states to Rāma, that wealth, pleasure and all things can be acquired by Dharma. It is the essence of the universe.[187] It is also stated in the Rāmāyaṇā that one who pursues Artha and Kāma in life falls in the sea of calamities. Rāma states to Lakṣamaṇa that if they pursue Artha or Kāma as the sole or supreme aim of life, great evil will result as it came in the life of the king Daśaratha.[188]

K. B. Iyer observes, in this regard, "The petty minded people pursue Dharma for the sake of wealth. But high minded ones pursue Dharma for the sake of purification of the mind. The Mahābhārata lays down that Dharma should be performed for the sake of Dharma only and not for the sake of enjoyment and desires. The only satisfaction is that one had done one's duty. Virtue is its own reward."[189] Maganlal A. Buch in his book 'The principles of Hindu Ethics' maintains that the sense of duty must be paramount over all considerations. If there is a conflict between duty and worldly good or duty and life, the former must be unhesitatingly preferred.[190]

Prof. M. Hiriyanna quoting Prabhākara treats Dharma as an end in itself. According to him, the idea of the Phala or the result to be attained, irrespective of its being for one self or for others, should be completely abandoned, and Dharma should be regarded as an intrinsic value, worth of being pursued for its own sake, what ought to actuate man in pursuing it is the consciousness that it is his duty do do so and never the prospect of satisfying any desire that he or others may have. Dharma accordingly becomes an ultimate value here and not merely an instrumental one. What is noteworthy is the total rejection of hedonistic stand-point and the replacement of it by the principle of duty for duty's sake.[191]

Here we are reminded of Kant's famous dictum of 'Duty for Duty's sake'. According to him also, we should not do anything for any reward of getting pleasure or avoiding pain. But we ought to perform our actions for duty's sake. For Kant, it is good in itself and considered by itself is to be esteemed much higher than all that can be brought about by it in favour of any inclination.[192]

Shridhar V. Katkar is also of the opinion that according to Hindu theory, even a person who feels doubtful regarding the existence of God or the life after death is still and must be a follower of Dharma. Though the theologians believed that life led according to the Principle of Dharma will lead to eternal bliss, they regarded it only as a probable result. Dharma according to them is to be followed for its own sake, and irrespective of any reward.[193]

But if we make a comprehensive study of the Mahābhārata, we find that Dharma is, in general, taken to be a means to Mokṣa than an end in itself. The ultimate end is liberation which is attained by a faithfull observance of Dharma.

According to the epic, Dharma is meaningful and valuable so far as it leads to liberation. In this connection Sivaswami Aiyar states that according to Hindu ethical thought, the ends of human actions are four. Dharma (duty or virtue), Artha (wealth), Kāma (pleasure and happiness or desire) and Mokṣa (salvation or emancipation). Of these four objects of human endeavour Dharma and Artha are not primary ends, or end in themselves, but are means to the other two ends, Kāma and Mokṣa are not means to other ends, but are regarded as ultimate ends. As between the two, Mokṣa is undoubtedly regarded as the summum bonum or the highest end.[194] He further adds that though Kāma is a primary end and Dharma and Artha are only secondary ends, they are also closely inter-dependent. The pursuit of Kāma or Artha by itself in contravention to Dharma or duty is forbidden. Wealth is desirable as a means to the performance of duty and the attainment of happiness. Secondary ends often become primary and Dharma, though secondary to the ultimate end of Mokṣa, has acquired a predominance in relation to the other ends.[195] Thus, we find that Dharma is given predominance over other ends but still it is regarded as secondary to liberation.

At several places in the epic, it is stated that by performing Dharma, the performer gets pleasure. When Yudhiṣṭhira asks Bhīśma to tell about Dharma whether whatever is done in this universe for the sake of pleasure is Dharma, or whatever is done for the sake of the other world, or whatever is done for the good of both the worlds in Dharma.[196] Bhīṣma then replies, "Ubhayatra sukhodarka iha caiva paratra ca" i.e. by performing Dharma pleasure is obtained both in this world and the other.[197] It is also stated "pretyabhāve Sukhaṁ dharmācchaśvatta-irupabhujyate," i.e., man always enjoys pleasure after death only with the help of Dharma.[198] So we fine that Dharma is placed as a means to attain happiness either in this world or in the other.

In the Śāntiparva, Tulādhāra teaches Dharma to Jājali as a means to attain Brahman and heaven. He thus says, "Dharma is fruitless and purposeless, its nature is very subtle, and Dharma has been explained only for attaining heaven and Bṛahman.[199] In the Anuśāsanaparva, Bṛhaspati states to Yudhiṣṭhira that the person who performs Dharma alone goes to heaven and he who does not perform Dharma goes to hell.[200] He further states that for this reason, wisemen should perform Dharma with the wealth acquired by justified means as Dharma alone is the means to heaven.[201] Again it is repeatedly mentioned in the same parva that with the help of Dharma individuals go to heaven.[202] In Bhārata sāvitri also Vyāsa lays emphasis on the performance of Dharma as from it both Artha and Kāma can be achieved.[203] Here Vyāsa himself regards Dharma as a means to satisfy desires and to get wealth.

Dr. T. M. P. Mahadevan does not regard Dharma as an end in itself. To him, it is a means to Mokṣa which is the final end.[204] He quotes the Gītā in his support. In the end of the Gītā, Kṛṣṇa asks Arjuna to relinquish all Dharmas and to seek refuge in God. He thus states, "surrendering all duties to me, seek refuge in Me alone. I shall absolve you of sins, grives not."[205]

Swami Sivananda states in this connection regarding Dharma as a means to salvation, "Dharma is given the foremost rank in the scriptures among the four puruṣartha, the grand object of human aspirations. Through Dharma, the other three,

Artha, Kāma and Mokṣa come automatically to you, because, through the practice of Dharma alone one can achieve his goal of life and crown himself with eternal bliss and supreme peace."[206]

We find severnal verses in support of the view that Dharma is an end in itself. But it does not appear consistent with the view which regards salvation as the highest and final goal of life. Only the highest goal can be an end in itself. We have also discussed that Dharma always brings about social unity, stability and progress. So, it should be regarded as a means and not as an end in itself. We have seen that Dharma is conducive to attainment of prosperity in this life and at the end to liberation. In both the cases, it is a means and not an end.

Reference

1. Vora, D. P., Evolution of morals in epics, p. 181.
2. Venkataraman, N, The Phil. Qty., Vol. VIII. No. 1-1932, p. 68
3. Sharma, I. C., Ethical Philosophy of India, p. 72.
4. Keith, A. B., Religion and Philosophy of the Veda, I, p. 38
5. Gokhale, B. G., Indian Thought Though the ages, p. 25
6. Radhakrishnan, S., Religion and Society, p. 157.
7. Keith, Religion and Philosophy of the Veda, II, p. 479; Gokhale, B. G. Indian Thought through the ages, p. 26.
8. Radhakrishnan, S., Indian Philosophy, I, p. 131
9. Radhakrishnan, S., Religion and Society, p. 107
10. Kane, P.V., History of Dharmaśāstra, Vol. 11, pt.1, p.5.
11. Ibid., Vol. 1, P. 1-2.
12. Ghoshal, U.N., A History of Indian political Ideas, P. 43.
13. Hopkins, E.W., Ethics of India, p. 192.
14. Maitra, S.K., Ethics of the Hindus P. 83
15. Raju, P.T., The Buddhistic Conception of Dharma, pub, in B.O.R.J. 1939-40, p.104.
16. Buch, M.A., The Principles of Hindu Ethics, P.52
17. Maitra, S.K., Ethics of The Hindus, P.82-83.

18. Ibid., P.87.
19. Ibid., P.81-82.
20. Jai - Sū, 1.1.2.
21. Iyer, K. Balasubramania, Yaksha Prashna. Foreword, P.VII,
22. Encyclopaedia of Religion and Ethies, edi. by James Hastings.
23. Mackenzie, John, Hindu Ethics, P. 38-39.
24. Drekmier, Charles, Kingship and Community in early India, P.8.
25. Ibid., P.6.
26. Ibid., P.9
27. P. Younger and S.O. Younger, Hinduism, P.37.
28. Zimmer, Heinrich, philosophies of India, p.41.
29. Mookerji, Radha Kumud, Ancient Indian Education, p.58.
30. Ibid., p. 268.
31. Ibid., p.150.
32. Aiyer, P. S, Sivaswami, Evolution of Hindu moral Ideals, p.6.
33. Ibid., p.13.
34. Bhattacharyya, H.D., The meaning of Dharma, Review of philosophy and Religion 7, No, 11, p. 43.
35. Ibid.
36. Gokhale, B.G., Indian Thought Through the Ages, p. 27
37. Kane, P. V., History of Dharmaśāstra, Vol.1, part, II p.2.
38. Das, Bhagvan, The Social Organisation, Vol.I, p.49.
39. Ibid., p. 50,
40. Karṇa, 90, 111-112.
41. Ibid. 91, 3-42.
42. Ibid, 69, 58.
43. Sukathankar, V.S, On the Meaning of the Mahābhārata, P.81.
44. Uttara, prakṣipta Sarga, 11, 7.
45. Śānti, 262, 6; Cri. edi. 251, 6.
46. Ibid, 262, 8-11; Cri. edi, 254, 9 and 11.
47. Ibid, 90, 40.
48. Ibid, 121, 40, 90, 3 and 5.

49. Vana, 33, 46.
50. Vana, 209, 2.
51. Gītā, 2, 31
52. Ibid., 8, 35.
53. Śānti, 21, 11-12.
54. Ibid 60, 7-8.
55. Vana , 313, 117.
56. Anu, 104, 155; , Maun, 1, 108.
57. Anu, 141, 65,
58. Vana, 206, 83.
59. Śānti, 35, 48.
60. Svargā, 5-32.
61. Śānti, 109, 10.
62. Karṇa, 69, 56,
63. Śānti, 259, 5.
64. Śānti, 270, 40; Cri. edi., 262, 37.38.
65. Mahābhārata paricaya, Gītā Press, p.68.
66. Mahadevan, T.M.P., The concept of Dhatma in the Mahābhārata, pub. in Vedant Kesari, may, 1950, P.19.
67. Siddhenathananda, Swami, some thoughts on Gita, pub. in Vedanta Kesari, November, 1961, P. 803.
68. Atreya, B. L. Bhartiya Nīti Śāstra Ka Etihasa, p. 159,
69. Vana, 2-74.
70. chap., 109, 12-13 ; 21, 11-12.
71. Śānti, 60, 7-8.
72. Ibid, 270, 39-40: Cri. edu., 262, 37-38.
73. Bāla, XIII, 12; XIV, 10.
74. Ibid, XVM, 30.
75. Ibid, XVIII, 50: Sued: I, 120.
76. Ibid, XXXIII, 7: XXXIII, 9, Sund. LV, 3 to 6.
77. Ayo, III, 42, 46,
78. Araṇyaka, LXIV, 55.
79. Ayo, XXI, 13.

80. Araṇyaka, XXXVII, 2.
81. Kiṣ, III, 32-34.
82. Ibid VIII, 8, 9, 40; XXXII, 7
83. Ibid VIII, 21.
84. Ayo, CIX, 1,2, 13 17, 21; Kiṣ., XIV, 14.
85. Ibid XXXIII 12, Kiṣ., XV, 19; Sund, XXXVIII, 14; Yuddh, XVIII, 27-34.
86. Kiṣ., XXXIII, 46; XXIV, 46; XXXIV, 12; Sund, I, 11
87. Ayo. LXXII 48, Ayo., CXVIII 5; Ayo, CXVIII, 6, Kiṣ., XYXIII, 34, Kis., VI, 21.
88. Sund, XI, 41
89. Ibid XII I, 47.
90. Ibid XXI, 9.
91. Ibid XXVI, 49-50
92. Ibid XLi,5-6.
93. Utt., LXXXIII, 20.
94. Sivananda, Swami, Ethical Teachings, p. 3.
95. Śānti, 259, 20-22
96. Ādi 11, 13.
97. Śānti, 109, 12.
98. Ibid, 262, 30; Cri. edi. 254, 20.
99. Anu, 113, 3.
100. Ibid, 115, 1 and 69.
101. Ibid, 116, 12.
102. Ibid, 116, 28-29.
103. Śānti, 162, 24
104. Śānti; 162, 4-5; Cri. edi. 156, 4-5.
105. Anu, 125, 59-88
106. Ādi, 74, 103.
107. Ibid, 74, 104-106.
108. Anu, 166, 49.
109. Vana, 29, 43.
110. Ibid, 29, 52.

111. Ibid, 29, 36-37.
112. Gītā, 16, 21.
113. Anu, 145, 54-55.
114. Ibid, 75, 14-15.
115. Śānti, 160, 10 and 15-16; Cri. edi. 154, 10 and 14-15.
116. Ibid, 160, 7-18 , Cri. edi. 154, 7-18.
117. Ibid, 26, 25-28
118. Ibid, 26, 31
119. Gītā 2, 62-63.
120. Udyoga, 43, 16.
121. Ādi, 79, 6,
122. Ketkar, Shridhar V., An Essay on Hinduism, P. 15.
123. Ibid, P. 16; Ādi, 114, 40.
124. Śānti, 145, 3.
125. Ibid, 5 and 4 1/2.
126. Kane, P.V., History of Dharmeśastra, Vol.II, Part-1, P. 16.
127. Ibid, P.3.
128. Vana, 207, 83; Arm, 141, 65.
129. Śānti, 60, 12.
130. Anu, 48, 12-13.
131. Śānti, 61: 8.
132. Ibid, 78. 2.
133. Ibid, 238, 87,
134. Ibid, 252, 4; Cri. edi., 260, 4.
135. Patanjali, Yogasūtra, 2, 31.
136. Ibid, 2, 30.
137. Gītā, 1, 36.
137. Droṇa, 190, 46-47.
139. Ādi, 11, 14.
140. Manu, 5, 81.
141. Śānti. 237, 3.
142. Śānti, 15, 26.

143. Ibid, 15, 20-21.
144. Vana, 207 to 216.
145. Ibid 208, 32 and 3 4.
146. Ibid, 209, 3.
147. Ibid, 209, 4.
148. Śānti, 36, 11.
149. Ibid, 109, 4.-5.
150. Ibid, 109, 1.
151. Karṇa, 69, 62.
152. Śānti, 329, 13.
153. Karṇa, 69, 33-34.
154. Ibid, 69, 32.
155. Śānti, 34, 25.
156. Karṇa 69, 29 to 521/2.
157. Vana, chap. 110-113.
158. Ibid, 122, 124.
159. Ādi, 104, 9-11.
160. Ibid, 105, 6-22.
161. Śānti, 141, 39.
162. Vana, 28. 6.
163. Ibid, 28, 7. and 13,
164. Ibid, 116, 14.
165. Śānti, 108, 18.
166. Ibid, 140, 48; 57, 7; Ādi, 139, 52.
167. Ibid, 33, 32; 78, 32; 260, 8; Cri. edi, 252, 8.
168. Ibid, Chap. 129 to 167, Cri. edi.; 131 to 173.
169. De, Sushil Kumar, The Mahābhāratda, History of Philosophy: Eastern and Western, edi. by Radhakrishnan and others, p. 9o,
170. Śānti, 78, 34.
171. Ibid, 294, 4; Cri, edi., 283, 3.
172. Śānti, 78, 2.
173. Ibid, 294, 4; Cri. edi., 283, 3.

174. Ibid, 242, 17-13, Cri. edi; 250, 17-19.
175. Gītā, 2, 47.
176. Śānti, 167, 7; Cri. edi., 151, 7.
177. Āśva, 31. 9.
178. Vana, 31, 2-5.
179. Ibid, 30, 5.
180. Ibid, 30, 6.
181. Ibid, 30, 7
182. Śānti, 167, 8-9.
183. Ibid, 181, 7; Cri. edi., 174, 7.
184. Vana, 33, 44.
185. Svargā, 563.
186. Udyoga, 40, 12-11; Cri, edi.
187. Araṇya, IX, 30.
188. Ayodhyā, 53, 8.
189. Iyer, Balasubramania K., Yaksha Prashna, P. XVII.
190. Buch, Maganlal A., The Principles of Hindu Ethics, P. 41
191. Hiriyanna, M,. The Indian Conception of Values' Pub. in Annals of Bhandarkar Oriental Research Journal, vol. 19, 1938-39, P. 14-15.
192. Abott, T.K., Kant's theory of Ethics, P. 10.
193. Ketkar, Shridhar V., An Essay on Hinduism, its fromation and future, p. 15.
194. Aiyar, Sivaswami P.S. Evolution of Hindu moral Ideals, P. 15.
195. Ibid.
196. Śānti, 259.2; Cri, edi. 250, 2.
197. Ibid, 258, 5; Cri, edi, 250, 4.
198. Ibid, 198, 33; Cri, edi, 187, 32.
199. Ibid, 262, 36; Cri. edi. 254, 35.
200. Anu, 111, 15-17.
201. Ibid, 16-17.
202. Ibid, 117, 26; and 24.
203. Svargā, 5, 62.

204. Mahadevan, T.M.P., The concept of Dharma in the Mahābhārata, pub, in Vedant Kesari, November, 1961, p. 21.
205. Gītā, 48, 66.
206. Sivananda, Swami, Ethical Teachings, p.6.

2

Social and Individual Ethics

The social and individual ethics are found in the scheme at Varṇāśramadharmas. Varṇadharmas are the duties relating to one's social class. The Āśramadharmas are the duties relating to one's specific stage of life. The Dharmas of both varṇa and aśrāma together constitute the code of duties-social and individual. The theory of varṇa or class emphasises the social aspect, and that of āśrama or stage of life, the individual aspect of ethics. The two aspects are however inseparably related or integrated together. As Pandharinath H. Valavalkar puts it, "Of course both the kinds of dharmas (Āśrama and Varṇadharma) concern themselves with the organisation and management of the individual as well as the group or the society; but difference may be said to be in the manner of approach and emphasis in the organisation of man and his activities in regard to the two kinds of dharmas. In the scheme of the stages, the problem is approached from the point of view of the training of the individual through specifically provided environment at different stages of his life; in the varṇa organization, on the other hand, the problem is considered from the point of view of the large group, and the individual's position is defined in this group with reference to his innate nature."[1] S. K. Maitra also observes, "The Varṇāśṛmadharmas thus represent a code of relative duties and constitute the relativistic ethics of the Hindus. It comprises the ethics of sociality as well as the ethics of individual capacity and is thus fuller and more comprehensive than the Platonic scheme which is the ethics of sociality only."[2]

We have defined earlier the distinction between general and specific Dharmas. Varṇāśramadharmas are specific as they do not cover the entire scope of moral life in the epic. Sādhāṛaṇadharmas come under the sphere of general ethics as they concern all individuals and being broader than Vaṛṇāśramadharma in scope, seem to constitute the foundation of the Varṇāśramadharma. But both of them are meant for the mutual protection, development, help and co-ordination among individuals.

Before dealing with Varṇadharmas, it is essential to distinguish between caste and class as they are often confused together and used almost synonymously. The reason of this is that the names of the four classes-Brāhman, Kṣatriya, Vaiśya and Śūdra are also the main divisions of castes. The meaning of the caste-system is analysed by Sir T. W. Holderness. He defines it as a system by which the accident of birth determines once for all the whole course of man's social and domestic relations. Throughout life he must eat, drink, dress, marry and give in marriage in accordance with the usages of the community in which he is born.[3] The essential features of the caste may be enumerated in the following way. First, the caste of an individual is determined by his birth. Secondly, once it is decided it is decided for ever. Thirdly, it is unchangeable. Fourthly, all the social and domestic relations like the mode of eating, drinking, marriage and other usages will be according to the caste in which he is born. According to Dr. Radhakrishnan the chief features of caste are: (1) Heredity. One cannot change one's caste. (2) Endogamy. Every member of a caste must marry a member of the same caste and may not marry outside it. (3) Commensal restrictions. Regulations are imposed regarding the acceptance of food and drink from members of other castes.[4] Thus according to him, there are three chief features of the caste-system. But P.V. Kane maintains them as five. He adds two more i.e. (4) occupation i.e., members of castes follow certain occupations and not other; (5) gradation of castes, some being at the top in the social scale and other being deemed to be so low that they are untouchable. Some others like senart add another characteristic, viz., the caste council with its chief having in meeting assembled among other matters the power to regulate the conduct of its members, to impose the penalties of fine or excommunication for lapses.[5]

On the other hand, the class of an individual was determined mainly by his character, quality and functions. It was determined by birth also but it lacked the rigidity of the caste. The class was sometimes liable to change. Class-system was originally a concept based on the division of labour or services. It was a vocational division, Mahadev Desai describes the features of the Varṇa-system as follows "(1) The division was entirely vocations, in order that each might serve the best interests of the organism. If men devoted themselves to tasks for which their character and aptitude best fitted them, they would be able to give their best to the community..... (II) The division had regard to the requirements of the then existing society and these were broadly divided into (a) intellectual and spiritual' (b) defence, (c) production of wealth by (1) intelligent economy and by (2) labour. Each requirement was assigned to be fulfilled by a class possessing the particular gift necessary for its fulfilment .... (III) Purity or virtue was the monopoly of one. Salvation was through the proper selfless performance of one's task ... (IV) The functions were hereditary because heredity is a law of nature, but there were no exclusive divisions."[6]

The distinction between caste and varṇa has also been made by P. V. Kane. To him, varṇa is a matter of race, culture, character and profession. He maintains, "The idea of varṇa was, as we have seen, based originally on race, culture, character and profession. It takes account mainly of the moral and intellectual worth of men and is a system of classes which appears more or less natural. The idea of varṇa even in the Smṛtis lays far more emphasis on duties on a high standard of effort for the community or society rather than on the rights and privileges of birth. The system of Jātis (castes) lays all emphasis on birth and heredity and tends to create the mentality of clinging to privileges without trying to fulfil the obligations corresponding to such privileges."[7]

On comparison of the features of caste-system and class-system, it can be said that they are not identical with each other. It is difficult to trace the origin of the caste-system. P.V. Kane states, "Not only is it impossible to hold that the origin of the modern complexity of the caste-system is to be traced back to one single cause, but it is difficult to accept that even all the origins that have been postulated by the several authors can adequately and satisfactorily explain the modern caste-system.[8] Moreover, it is a fact that due to vested interest of some people or groups of people, the caste-system was brought into prevalence. S.V. Ketkar blames the Brāhmiṇ class for its origin.[9] Swami Dharma Theerthaji also considers priests responsible for the growth of the above system. He says, "Caste originated, quite in a different way, developed entirely on other lines, served completely another purpose, but the priests who helped its growth have tacked it on to the ancient names and ideals to justify it in the eyes of the people and cover up its inherent wickedness."[10]

Sometimes complexities in life and growth of population are also regarded responsible for the origin of this caste-system. Swami Nikhilanand is of the opinion that as the population increased and other complexities set in, the qualities of the individual became less easy to determine and heredity was gradually accepted as a sort of working principle to determine the caste.[11]

Apart from complexities in social life and growth of population, the indifferent attitude of the deciding authorities towards this system may be one of the reasons which facilitated the growth of present caste-system. To decide one's social class on the basis of birth is very convenient on the one hand and on the other the complexity involved in deciding an individual's class on the basis of conduct being tedious might have helped the fast growth of present caste-system.

Before coming to Varṇadharma directly, it is essential to study the history of the development of the class-organisation. According to Romesh Chandra Dutt, caste system did not exist in the Vedic period. He writes: "There is positive proof, and various passages in the Ṛgveda show that the caste-system did not exist. The very word varṇa which in later sanskrit indicates caste, is used in the Ṛgveda to distinguish the Aryan and the non-Aryans, and nowhere indicates separate sections in the Aryan community (III, 34, 9 and C). The very world 'Kṣatriya' which in later sanskrit means the military caste, is used in the Veda simply as an adjective which means strong and is applied to gods (VII, 64, 2; VII, 89, I and C). The very word 'Vipra', which in later sanskrit means the priestly caste, is used in Ṛgveda merely as an adjective which is applied to gods (VII, 11, 6 and C). And the very word 'Brahman', which in later sanskrit means also the priestly caste, is used in a hundred places in the Ṛgveda to imply the composer of hymns, and nothing else (VII, 103, 8 and C)."[12]

Narmadeshwar Prasad observes that the caste system was not established in the vedic period when society was not stable, and was still migrating to have hereditary, exclusive social groupings,"[13] Again at another place he states, "There was no caste-system in this period. There were not the conditions which go to build up the institution of caste-system. The different classes inter-married among themselves without any restrictions. We hear of the Kṣatriya Raja Rathabithi giving his daughter to a Brahman Sakasva (Vājasaneyi Saṁhitā - XXIII, 31). The Brahman Bṛhaspati giving his daughter Romasa to the Kṣatrīya king Savaneya Bhavagavya (Taittiriya Saṁhita, VII, 4, 19. 3). We also get cases of union between twice-born men and Sūdra, (Vājasaneyi Saṁhitā, XXIII, 31), and Śūdramen and women of the twice-born classes (Ibid. XXIII, 32). Not even there was any restriction on inter-dining to be found in the Vedas."[14]

A contrary view is held by G. S. Ghurye. He observes, "In the Ṛgveda, the earliest literature of the first period, three classes of society are very frequently mentioned, and named Brahman, Kshatriya, and Viś- The first two represented broadly the two professions of the poet-priest and the warrior-chief. The third division was apparently a group comprising all the common people."[15] He further observes in this connection, "It is only in one of the later hymns, the celebrated 'Puruṣa sukta', that a reference has been made to four orders of society as emanating from a sacrifice of the primeval being. The names of those four orders are given there as Brāhmana, Rājanya, Vaīśya, and Śūdra, who are said to have come respectively from the mouth, the arms, the thighs and the feet of the creator. "[16] Dr. S. Radhakrisnan also mentions that the first reference to it is in the Puruṣa Sukta, where the different sections of society are regarded as limbs of the great self.[17]

The post-Vedic period had the tradition and back-ground of the class-stuggle between the Brāhimiṇs and the Kṣatriyas. It was in this period that King Vena disallowed the priest to make sacrifices, king Puruvas despoiled the Brāhmiṇs of their ornaments, king Nahuṣa forcel one thousand Brāhmiṇs to draw his chariot, etc.[18]

Coming to the epic era we get a clear picture of this class-system. In the Rāmāyaṇa, it was not in a marked shape. In this connection Narmadeshwar Prasad writes, "In the Rāmāyaṇa,

Brahman earned his livelihood by digging the earth with spades and ploughs. But later on, in the Mahābhārata age, a Brahman could not carry on such a 'mean' profession"[19] K.S. Ramaswami Sastri holds the view that in the Rāmāyaṇa the four caste (Chaturvarṇa) ideals had been firmly established.[20] The references of the varṇas are found on many occasions in the Rāmāyaṇa. In the Bālakāṇḍa Viśvāmitra states to Rāma that mercy should not be shown even in killing women for the benefits of four varṇas.[21] In the Kiṣkindhākṇḍa also we get the reference to this effect.[22]

There are many other passages relating to four varṇas but they do not imply any demand of rights and privileges. Sastri observes: "Though the Brāhmaṇas were the foremost group and though the Śūdras could not study the Vedas (Sundra, XXVIII, 5), yet the utmost harmony prevailed among all the social groups (Bāla, VI, 19), and all were devout hospitable, greatful, noble, valorous, and full of heroism."[23] In the Rāmāyaṇa we find that on certain occasions all people were fed without any exclusion[24] Romesh Chandre Dutt is of the opinion that the great distinction between the society of the Vedic times and the society of the epic period was that caste-system was unknown in the former and had gone up in the latter.[25] K.M. Sen also has the same opinion. But with slight difference he observes, "Incidentally, while the epics show a hardening of the caste system, which was not strong in the Vedic days, they also certain a remarkable number of heroes from the lower castes. Vidura, one of the wisest men at the court of the Kurus, is the son of a Śūdra maid servant. The proud Brāhmiṇ Kauśika is humbled by the religious butcher of Mithilā (Vaṇa 206, 14). In fact the author (or compiler) of the Mahābhārata is himself described as the son of a fisherman[26]. Thomas also confirms the above view by adding the name of Karṇa who was born illegitimate and was brought up by a low-born charioteer.[27]

It is obvious from the above that there was class system in the epic era and not the caste system. D. P. Vera, in this connection, differentiates between varṇa and caste. "The Epics", he observes, "deal with the varṇas and not castes. Evidently the stratification of the society then was less complex than that of the modern one. Yet in the final recast of the Mahābhārata, the Varṇa system is found to be almost rigid with a regularity, established social hierarchy formed on the basis of birth. The epics, in agreement with the other Hindu religious literatures, accept the divine origin of the varṇa stratification, but conscious of the injustice involved in such a stratification, formed merely on the ground of birth, they soon try to justify it on other considerations."[28]

Coming to the Mahābhārata in particular, we find a picture of this four-fold varṇas in the Parāśaragītā. It is discussed very elaborately with distinctive duties. In the Parāśaragītā, Parāśara defines the respective duties of the fourfold varṇas in these words, 'A Brāhmin should live on alms, teaching, officiating as priest at other men's sacrifices. A Kṣtriya should protect his subjects, a Vaiśya should engage himself in agriculture, cattle-rearing and business and a Śūdra should serve the three orders.[29] At another place their duties are elaborated by Parāśara thus, "Thus Brāhmiṇs must show their proficiency in controlling their senses, Kṣatrīyas in victory in war, Vaiśya in acquiring wealth with justice, and Śūdras in serving."[30] Thus, it seems that in the epic period, society is divide into four orders and their duties are very distinctively separated from one another.

In order to know the Varṇa system fully, it is proper to study the details of the respective duties of the four varṇas. In this four-fold scheme of the class system, Brāhmiṇs are the highest class whose sole aim is to acquire knowledge and learning and lead a well-disciplined and ascetic life of purity and simplicity. In the great epic, Lord Maheśvara, describing the duties of the

Brāhmiṇ to his wife Umā, observes, "To perform sacrifice and officiating as priest at other men's sacrifices, gift-making and acceptance of gift, to study the Vedas and to teach the Vedas to others are the only six duties of a Brāhmiṇ"[31]

The duties of the Brāhmiṇ are divided into three Kinds. Study of the Vedas is treated as the primary duty, performing sacrifices as the eternal and offering gift according to capacity as the excellent duty.[32] Yudhiṣṭhīra mentions to the Serpent some other duties like veracity, gift, austerity and mercy.[33] There duties are also maintained by the religious butcher to the Brāhmin.[34]

Next to Brāhmiṇ, the class of Kṣatriya comes. In the epic, Bhīṣma enlists protection of the people, gift-making, performance of sacrifices, study of the Vedas and abstention from luxury, in general, as the duties of Kṣatriyas.[35] Again they are mentioned in chapter 40 of the Udyogaparva and chapter 186 of the Śāntiparva. The fundamental function of the Kṣatriyas is the protection of people. No doubt, the role of the Brāhmiṇs is very exalted, but as a matter of fact the Kṣatriys are supposed to uphold the organization of society.

In the epic, a Kṣatriya is not admired for his mere physical strength alone. He is not only the embodiment of force but his life is also for right and justice. The force is to be applied in the service of right. Bhīṣma states, "That Kṣatriya is said to be acquainted with his duty, who slays in battle-field his very preceptors, if they happen to be sinful, and covetous and disregardful of restraints and vows."[36] Nārada states in the Droṇaparva that the duties of the Kṣatriyas are in correspondence with the name which stands for protection of people from wounds and injuries.[37] The word 'Kṣatriya' comes from the word 'Kṣi' which means to possess, to have power over, to rule, govern, to be master of, etc. And the word 'Kṣatriya' means governing, endowed with sovereignty.[38] Thus, here also their duties come from their name of class.

The third is the merchant class known as Vaiśya varṇa. The duties of the Vaiśyas are described as ploughing, cattle-rearing and trading. This class is not less important than the other two higher classes of society. They are the real foundation of the whole social economy. They may be said to be the business community of the Hindu society. In the Śāntiparva, the duties of the Vaiśyas are mentioned by Bhiśma as gift, study of the Vedas, sacrifices and accumulation of wealth by fair means.[39] It is obvious that the main duties of the Vaiśyas besides gifts are, study and sacrifices, to devote themselves to cattle-rearing, growing of crops, storing grains, business and trade.[40] this is stated by Bhṛgu to Bhardvāja. So, it a class of agriculturists and businessmen.

Last comes the varṇa of the Śūdra. Bhīṣma says in the Śāntiparva that Prajāpati has created the Śūdras to be the servants of these three classes. Hence, to serve all three classes is the prescribed duty of the Śūdras by the Śāstras.[41] The same is mentioned in the Parāśaragītā,[42] As Louis Renou puts it, the Śūdra is one, "who is habitually addicted to all kinds of food, performs all kinds of work, who is unclear, who has abandoned the Vedas, and does not practise pure observances, is traditionally called a Śūdra."[43] Similar descriptions regarding the Śūdra have been given in the epic by saint Bhṛgu.[44]

In the Śāntiparva, Bhīṣma maintains that a Śūdra has no property of his own and that he cannot accumulate any kind of property of his own.[45] But it is also stated by Parāśara that if a Śūdra fails to get his livelihood by serving these three calsses, then he is permitted to earn his bread and butter by trading, cattle-rearing and agriculture.[46] The Śūdras are also allowed to practise the duties of other varṇas. A Śūdra is also allowed to practise the duties of other varṇas. A Śūdra who takes to righteous courses of action comes very near to the other orders. Bhīṣma states, "For a Śūdra who is desirous of hearing such scriptures as are not forbidden to his case, who has accomplished his duties, who has begotten a son, between whom and the superior orders there is not much difference in consequence of the purity of his conduct, all the modes of life have been laid down excepting the observance of universal peacefulness, and self-restraint (which are not necessary for him). For a Śūdra practising all these duties, as also for a Vaiśya, and a Kṣatriya, the bhikṣu (mendicancy) mode of life has been laid down."[47] Having observed the above facts regarding the duties of the Śūdras, it must be accepted that the Śūdras have a right to come nearer to the higher order by the performances of right conduct.

Thus, the educationists and the priests, the warriors and the political men, the agriculturists and businessmen and the unskilled labourers and servicemen form the four-fold varṇa system in society. The different functions of social life seem to be distinctively separated. Each and every order has its own social aim and duties. It will be significant to note here that the functions of the different orders are treated as equally significant to the well-being of society. The wisdom and austerity of the Brāhmiṇs, the administration and bravery of the Kṣatriyas, the commercial and farming acumen of the Vaiśyas and the labour and service of the Śūdras are jointly taken to promote the social growth and well-being.

In the epic era, it appears from the above facts that society was an organic whole and thus there was an organic synthesis and mutual co-operations among the four varṇas as the different limbs of an organism. They were complementary to each other. Without their mutual co-ordination, the existence and prosperity of the social order was not possible. Hence, Manubhai C. Pandya very rightly compares society and its four classes to the limbs of a living being. The four classes are very useful limbs of the social organism whose existence, health and growth depend on their sound health and mutual co-operations. To him, mutual good-will, harmony, and co-operation are the very gist of the theory of caste."[48] Pandarinath H. Valavalkar also holds the same view as he writes, "In fact, the entire varṇa scheme as divised to co-ordinate and assemble the best and the utmost of group welfare, by yoking each section of the group on to duties and responsibilities in terms of the efficiency of specific work and service each of the sections is able to render unto the community life."[49]

Now we will discuss the question in the light of the Mahābhārata whether the varṇa system is based on birth or on character. There are several theories propounded in the Mahābhārata in relation to this question.

In the epic, we find traditional theory of divine origin of the class system. About the origin of the classes of Brāhmin, Kśatriya, Vaiśya and Śūdra, the epic relates to a story that all these four varṇas originated from the four limbs of God-mouth, arms, thigh and legs respectively. In the Śāntiparva when the Janaka asks Parāśara to tell him about the origin of the class system, Parāśara replies, "They that are conversant with the scriptures know that when the Lord of creatures set himself to create the worlds, some creatures sprang from his mouth, some from his arms, some from his thighs, and some from his feet. They that thus sprang from his mouth, O child, came to be called Brāhmiṇs. They that sprang from his arms were named Kṣatriyas. They, O king, that sprang from his thighs were the wealthy class called the Vaiśyas. And, lastly, they that were born of his feet were the serving class, viz., the Śūdras."[50] However, as a matter of fact the story, that the different classes sprang from the different limbs of God is a symbol which represents the different social functions of the four orders. It indicates that there are four main aspects of social work which are represented in the universe by four varṇas. G. S. Ghurye in this connection observes, "The Brahmins are declared to be chief because they were created from the mouth, punning as the worl 'Mukha' (mouth and chief)."[51] M.A. Buch states that the Kṣatriyas are the arms; that is, they from the military class, the Vaiśyas are the belly and the thighs; that is, the economic functions belong to them; and the Śūdras are the legs; that is they form the army of labourers.[52] So, these different names are due to their respective functions.

In the epic, at one place, colour is also introduced as another basis of the class-system by Bhṛgu. He states, "The complexion the Brāhmiṇs obtained was white, that which the Kṣatriyas obtained was red; that which the Vaiśyas got was yellow: and that which was given to the śūdras was black."[53] But he himself on being questioned by Bharadvāja about its instinctive nature as the basis of class distinction changes his view at once. He thus states, "In the beginning there was no caste system, and naturally all were Bhāhmiṇs and the different varṇas came into existence only due to their actions."[54] Thus, the propounder of the colour theory does not maintain it and shifts immediately to the functional basis of varṇa. It is based on the nature of occupation which a person selects. It is proved from the story of Viśvāmitra narrated by Nārada in the Udyogaparva. Viśvāmitra was not allowed to rise to the higher order of Brāhmiṇhood till he suppressed his lust and wrath. It was only when he mastered his self completely that he became a Brāhmiṇ.[55] In the epic, the degradation of the performances and character of a Brāhmiṇ carries with it a corresponding degradation in his status. It is declared by Bhīṣma in the Śāntiparva that those names which are applied among men to slaves and dogs and wolves, and (other) beasts, are also applied to the Brāhmiṇ, who is engaged in pursuits that are improper for him.[56] Bhīṣma states that a wretched Brāhmiṇ, who falls away from his duties, and whose behaviour is wicked, becomes a Śūdra. The Brāhmiṇ, who marries a Śūdra women, who becomes vile in conduct, or a dancer or a village servant, or does other improper acts, becomes equal to a Śūdra, and on such occasions of feeding, he should be assigned a place among

Śūdras.[57] Hence the generic title of a Brāhmiṇ does not carry much importance. It is essential to consider the character or the performances of the person who claims for Brāhmiṇhood.

In the Gītā, it is found that class system is also based on guṇa (qualities) and Karma (functions). In this connection, Kṛṣṇa declares, "Cāturvarnyaṁ mayā sṛṣtaṁ guṇakarmavibhāgaśaḥ i.e., I myself have created the arrangement of the four classes (into Brāhmiṇs, Kṣatriya, Vaiśyas, and Śūdras), consistently with the differences in their qualities and actions.[58] In the 18th chapter the gives the detailed description of duties of these four Varṇas according to their inherent nature or prakṛti. Here the three ingredients of prakṛit viz., sattva, rajas and tamas, which are manifested in all created being in varied proportion have been taken into account.

The opinions of the ancient seers seem to be that it is not birth, nor any other quality which determines a man's varṇa, but his actions, habits, and character are deciding factors. In the Śantiparva a Fox states, "My birth has been low. It is conduct, however, that determines the race."[59] Again it is observed by Maheśvara that a Śūdra attains to a superior colour of Brāhmiṇhood by righteous acts.[60] In the Vanaparva Yudhiṣṭhira laying emphasis on action replies to Yakṣa "Listen, O Yakṣa! it is neither birth, not study, nor learning, that is the cause of Brāhmiṇhood. Without doubt it is behaviour that constitutes it."[61] It is quite more obviously shown in the Anusāśanaparva when Maheśvara states, "One that is a Brāhmiṇ, when he becomes wicked in conduct and observes no distinction in respect of food, falls away from the status of Brāhmiṇhood, and becomes a Śūdra. Even a Śūdra that has purified his soul by pure deeds, and that has subjugated all his senses, deserves to be waited upon and served with reference as a Brāhmin. This has been said by the self-born Brahmā himself. When a pious nature and pious deeds are noticeable even in a Śūdra, he should, according to my opinion, be held superior to a person of the three regenerate classes. Neither birth, nor the purificatory rites, nor learning, nor offspring, can be regarded as grounds for conferring upon one the status of regeneracy (Dvijatva). Verily, conduct is the only ground. All Brāhmins in this world are Brāhmiṇs in consequences of conduct ..... The boon-giving Brāhmā, while he created all creatures, himself said that the distribution of human beings into four orders as dependent on birth is only for purpose of classification. "[62] In the Parāśaragītā, Parāśara regards a Virtuous Śūdra as effulgent Viṇnu of the universe, the foremost one in all the worlds."[63]

The discourse between the Serpent and Yudhiṣṭhira throws ample light on the subject. Yudhiṣṭhira says, "those characteristics that are present in a Śūdra, do not exist in a Brāhmiṇ; nor do those that are in a Brāhmiṇ exist in a Śūdra. And a Śūdra is not a Śūdra by birth alone-nor a Brāhmin in Brāhmin by birth alone. He, it is said by the wise, in whom are seen those virtues, is a Brāhmiṇ. And people term his a Śūdra, in whom those qualities do not exist, even though he be a Brāhmin by birth.[64] He goes ahead to state, "In human society, O mighty and highly intelligent Serpent, it is difficult to ascertain one's caste, because of the promiscuous intercourse among the four order. This is my opinion. Men belonging to all the orders (promiscuously) begot offspring upon women of all the orders. And of men, speech, sexual intercourse, birth and death are common. And to this the Ṛṣis have borne testimony, by using at the beginning of a sacrifice, such expressions as, of what caste soever we may be, we celebrate the sacrifice. Therefore, those that are wise have asserted that character is the chief essential requisite."[65] He says in the end of the discourse, "O excellent Snake, whosoever now conforms to the rules of pure and virtuous conduct, him have I, ere now designated as a Brāhmiṇ."[66]

In the Rāmāyaṇa also, the emphasis is laid upon the

character to determine, the varṇa of the individual. Rāma states to jābāli thus; "one's character (fashioned according to scripture) shows whether one is high-born or base, heroic or vainly priding himself on his manliness, pure or impure."[67]

Thus, the morality expressed in 'Varṇadharma' or duties relating to four classes, is the morality which follows the division of labour, occupations and performances which people had in society. Sir Gokul Chand Narang says, "The fact that in its origin caste was determined by one's occupation is not only a matter of historical proof but is also shown by the process which during comparatively recent centuries led to the growth of sub-castes."[68] I.C. Sharma also bases this varṇa system on personality and character but not on birth and religious distinctions. According to him the Śūdras form the body, the Vaiśyas the mind, the kṣatiyas the intellect and the Brāhmiṇs the soul of the social organism.[69]

J. C. Nesfield regards occupation as the exclusive basis of caste distinction. Caste, he regards, as a nature product of society int he creation of which religion played no part at all.[70] Dahlmann accepts division of Indian society originally into three groups which is natural and is found in every civilized community.[71]

Dr. Radhakrishnan opines that caste was the answer of Hinduism to the forces pressing on it from outside. It was the instrument by which Hinduism civilized different tribes it took in.[72] He further observes about the origin of varṇa system in these words, "caste on its social side is a product of human organisation and not a mystery of divine appointment. It is an attempt to regulate society with a view to actual difference and ideal unity."[73] R. N. Dandekar also says in the same manner, "Each caste is an independent social unit, guarding its members and customs, opposing other castes, but it is the peculiarity of the Hindu society that it integrates several such independent units into an organic whole."[74] V. R. R. Dikshitar observes that by fixing up a social structure of four castes on an organic basis, the ancient Hindus realised a well planned social economy where there would be no competition, no rivalry, no jealousy and no discontent.[75] Thomas expresses his feeling about this varṇa system in these words, "By defining every one's scope of activities in society, it eliminated the undesirable competitive spirit which is the curse of modern communities, and tended to cultivate a co-operative spirit between the several castes that inhabited a village or town."[76] Mackenzie views the varṇa system as an asset. In this regard he states that in a restless age in which the whole structure of western society is in danger of being reduced to chaos, it is not strange that the eyes of many should be directed to the more stable conditions that govern Hindu society, where each man has his place and function irrevocably assigned to him."[77] Emile Senart state "The caste is, to my mind, the normal continuation of ancient Aryan institutions taking their form according to the variations of conditions and environment which they encountered in India. "[78] C. V. Vaidya rightly remarks that neither in the past nor in the present age of world history, neither in the East nor in the West, has any country except the country of the Hindus developed that intricate social organization, which is known as caste,[79] Dr. Brij Gopal Tiwari tries to justify this varṇa system in line with modern principles of socialism and communism. He states, "its essence lies rather in the recognition of an organic community, fraternity. From this view-point, even the socialist principle of payment according to need or capacity and more so, the communist principle of payment according to need, would be in line with the principle of varṇa, the idea of an organic commonalty has, indeed, according to social psychologists, a great part to play in the coming age; and this progressive idea of an organic community represents, to our mind, the essence of the scheme of varṇa"[80].

Summarizing this social morality, we can say that the organization of classes was a social institution based on the principle of division of labour. In it each and every class was assigned certain occupation. Its members were asked to follow it in the best manner. They worked doing good to society and had mutual co-operation among the varṇas without any ill-will or rivalry or competition among them.

Now let us come to Āśramadharma. The life of the individual was divided into four stages or āśramas' i.e., Brahmacaryāśrama, Gṛhasthāśrama, Vānaprasthāśrama and Saṁnyāsāśrama. The duties of the individual, which were determined by the different stages are very elaborately discussed in the epic. The Brahmacaryāśrama may be called the stage of the students, the Gṛhasthāśrama - the stage of the householders, the Vānaprasthāśrama - the stage of the hermits residing in the forest away from cities and villages, and the Saṁnyāsāśrama the stage of ascetics leading a wandering life for spiritual enlightenment and salvation.

The word 'Āśrama' is originally derived from the Sanskrita root 'śrama' to exert oneself; therefore, it may mean, by derivation, (i) a place where exertions are performed, and (ii) the action of performing such exertions.[81] According to P.H. Valavalkar, "literally, an āśrama is a housing or resting place'. The word, therefore, signifies a halt, a stoppage or a stage in the journey of life just for the sake of, in a sense, rest in order to prepars oneself for further journey. The āśramas, then, are to be regarded as resting places during one's journey on the way to final liberation which is the final aim of life"[82] Stages, as halting places in the journey of life, seem to be more logical and convincing because we ourselves feel that we have different obligations in different stages of our life. We should perform only those duties which are prescribed for the particular period of life. A man belongs to one particular stage for a limited period. One cannot proceed from one stage to another according to one's own choice without caring for one's age which is the guiding factor of these stages. So, a man has to wait at one stage till his age permits him for the change of the stage from one to another.

The stage of the student is a period of learning and discipline. After initiation, the boy goes to a teacher called as 'guru' from whom he receives instructions and education. For the whole period, he lives with his teacher in a position of subordination to him. It has a significance because it moulds and forms the boy's character. Here, a strict moral education is given to the boys. Saint Bhṛgu narrates the duties of the student-life thus, "He who is in this mode of life, should have his soul cleansed by purity of conduct, by Vedic rites, and by restrains and vows and humility. He should worship the morning and evening twilights, the sun, his own sacred fire, and the deities. He should perform his ablutions thrice, (viz., in the morning, noon, and evening). He should lead a life of celibacy: attend to his sacred fire; dutifully serve his preceptor; daily go out on a round of mendicancy (for supporting himself); and give ungrudgingly unto his preceptor the whole of what is obtained in alms. Willingly accomplishing everything that the commands of his preceptor may indicate, he should be ready to receive such Vedic instruction as his preceptor may give him as a favour."[83] In another context the same duties have been mentioned by Maheśvara in the Anuśāsanaparva.[84]

When we analyse these duties mentioned in the epic, the life of a student seems to be the embodiment of these ethical elements of service, study, simplicity, self-control, self-sacrifice, obedience, physical and moral courage and endurance.

Service is the duty towards God, the teacher and the parents. The service to be rendered to God is worship. In the Śāntiparva Bhīṣma suggests that a student should always keep himself in service to his teacher.[85] The main task of this stage is to study the Vedas and to know the nature of God, self, and world. Without them no one can judge actions as right or wrong and cannot choose the right path in life. Simple life is the important aspect of this stage. He does not get luxurious cloth, bed and food at all. He has to live on the food which he receives as alms. A student whether he is a prince or a pauper must obey the orders of his teacher. He has to obey the order without any exceptions. The qualities of physical capacity and moral courage are important characteristics of this stage. Only by his endurance, one can face the difficulties and calamities which fall upon him in life. Brachmacarya or control of the the mind and sense-organs is the essential virtue of this stage. This stage is named after this very virtue. Absolute chastity, absolute celibacy and absolute continence are necessary for student life. It seems to be based on sound psychological and moral reasons. During adolescence, all the vital energy of the youth is required for his physical and psychological development.

Annie Besant very nicely concludes the ethical elements of Brahmacaryāśrma in this way, "Sometimes in England the phrase is used 'the three R's and by this is meant the elements of education-Reading, Writing, and Arithmetic. To teach the three R's is to give a child elementary education. So we might call the elements of the Brahmacāri's life 'the four S's-Service, Study, Simplicity, and Self-control."[86]

The second stage is the life of a householder. The duties of this stage are also discussed very elaborately in the epic. The life of the householder comes when the student-life is completed. In this stage he weds a wife and produces children. The following description of duties has been given by Maheśvara in the Anuśāsaṇaparva, "To perform the five great sacrifices, namely the sacrifice to the Devas or Deities or gods, to the *Rṣis* or saints, to the Pitṛs or dead forefathers, to the men coming to the house and to the lower beings like cattle around and to keep the mind pure, are the duties of the householder. The householder is righteous who always speaks the truth, never sees the fault in others, offers gifts, respects the Brāhmiṇs, keeps his own house neat and clean, gives up vanity and pride, lives with humbleness, speaks affectionately or politely, engages himself in the services of guests, eats grains residued from sacrifices, and offers footwears, water, seat, bed, light and shelter to the guests in accordance with the orders of the scriptures."[87] Bhīṣma also enlists these duties in Śāntiparva. He further adds that the householder should remain satisfied with his wife with full affection and should have sensual gratification in proper time. He must meet the food and other requirements of the different stages.[88]

Observing the difference duties of the householder, we may briefly sum up the different ethical elements of this stage as service, study, simplicity, self-control,. diligence, self-restraint, sacrifices, courtesy, hospitality, tenderness and protection. They have been regarded as fundamental virtues for the householder.

This stage is regarded as very important because of its philanthropic scope. The whole world has to depend on it for food, lodging and clothing. In the Parāśaragītā, Parāśara states, "The other three stages are maintained by the householder."[89] It is most important also because the individual enters society with different responsibilities towards wife, father, mother, family, village and people at large. As I.C. Sharma puts it, "The Grihastha Asrama, or the order of the householder, is regarded as the most, important because it is at this stage that the individual enters the first unit of society, i.e., the family, and the responsibility of supporting his wife and children falls on him. As a husband and a father, he must experience love and utilize the wealth he earns for the fulfilment of his desires as well as those of his family members."[90]

The third stage of life is called the stage of the hermit. A man after completing the household life, taking firm resolution and keeping his sense-organs under control enters the forest-life. In the epic, Maheśvara suggests that the hermits should live in the forest, walk on the path of the forest and should lead their lives in the shelter of the forest like the teacher or guru.[91] In the Śāntiparva, Bhṛgu prescribes that a hermit should eat limited spontaneous grown grain, roots with leaves, give up beautiful clothes, tasteful food and sensual gratification of the householders in the villages.[92] Maheśvara enumerates the duties of the hermits as performing ablutions thrice a day, pouring libations to the sacred fires, observing of the excellent ordinances relating to yoga, sitting in summer in the midst of four fires on four sides with sun overhead, lying on bare rocks or the earth, exposing themselves to cold, water and fire and clothing themselves with barks of trees or deerskins.[93] In this stage, the individual does not altogether retire from social or family life. But he entrusts the entire responsibility of the household management to his younger generations. He devotes his time to the study of the holy scriptures and meditation. His wife may accompany him in his mission. At times he is consulted by the members of his family. He may continue to give them guidance in worldly matters in accordance with Dharma. Bhīṣma says that a hermit is permitted by the epic to live with his wife but the cannot have sensual gratification.[94] Thus we find that life becomes more and more rigorous and the lust to cling to the objects of pleasure of the world vanishes from the mind. So, hospitality, self-control and renunciation of worldly objects are the highlights of the ethical values found in this stage. This stage is the third stopping stone to the highest goal of salvation by renunciation observed by the Ascetic.

The fourth and the last order of life is that of the Ascetic who completely renounces his house, wife, children, wealth and everything. He lives as an ascetic abandoning all sorts of attachment to earthly objects. First the individual has to get rid of the sins committed by him by leading a well-disciplined and pure life to qualify himself for entering the stage which entails the supreme amount of self-sacrifice. In the Santiparva, Bhṛgu narrates in detail the duties of the Ascetic thus, "Freeing themselves from attachment to the sacred fire, wealth, spouse and children, and robes, seats, beds and such other objects of enjoyment, and breaking the bonds of affection, they roam about, regarding with an equal eye a clump of earth or enjoyment of the triple aggregate. They cast an equal eye on foes and friends and neutrals or strangers. They never injure, in thought, word, or deed, immobile things or creatures that are viviparous, or oviparous or born on filth or called vegetables. They have no homes. They roam over hills and mountains, upon shores of rivers or seas, under shades of trees, and among temples of deities. They may go to towns or villages for residence. In a town, however, they should not live for more than five nights, while in a village their residence should never exceed one night. Entering a town or a village, they should, for the support of life, repair to the adodes of only Brāhmiṇs of liberal deeds. They never ask for any alms except what is thrown into the (wooden) bowls they carry. They should free themselves from lust, wrath, pride, cupidity, delusion, miserliness, deceit, slander, vanity, and in jury to living creatures."[95]

Thus we see that this state of renunciation is reached only when the individual has enjoyed the last three states and is well inspired to go in quest of the ultimate reality. This is the life devoted entirely to the attainment of salvation. It is the ultimate life because the individual devotes his entire time to learning scriptures, discussing the nature of the ultimate reality and meditating on to have communion with it. Thus, the highlights of the ethical element of this stage is complete renunciation of the worldly life to achieve liberation.

In this connection, it must be mentioned, that the four ideals of human endeavour which we have discussed earlier are in consonance with these āśramas. Dharma, the first ideal of human efforts is accepted as the ideal of the first stage. Similarly the wealth and desire are recognized as the ideals of the second stage. In the third and the last stage liberation is found supreme. So, we find that these four ideals are related to these four stages.

Radha Kumud Mookerji gives a graphic description of this fourfold stage-system. By using a metaphor he treats the different stages of life as mutuality related in the same way as the bud, the flower and the fruit are related. The tender youth is first subjected to process of rigorous discipline and training. With a sound mind in a sound body, the budding youth blossoms into a noble manhood. The experience of an active life ripens into the fruit of mature, wisdom and moral steadfastness.[96]

Dr. Radhakrishnan also advocates the necessity of this fourfold stage system for perfect human life. He observes, "Every state is necessary and in so far as it is necessary it is good. The blossom does not deny the leaf and the leaf does not deny the stalk and the stalk the root."[97] Dr. Brij Gopal Tiwari justifies the scheme of āśramas on the basis of modern knowledge of child and industrial psychology. He says, "As regards the Āśrama principle, the investigations of modern researches in child psychology and the psychology of adolescence amply support the Indian system of physical, mental and moral development and of mental hygiene.[98]

It cannot be denied that the organization of the four āśrams of life is established for the gradual ethical and metaphysical sublimation of an individual. The fourfold division of human life is in accordance with the man's biological growth. As a matter of fact, the first stage is the period of training and discipline. It seems to be essential for the preparation of the life of the plastic youth to a life of responsibility. The next stage is the period of the householder. It supports the entire world by the performance of reciprocal duties, obligations and responsibilities. It is a period of practice and performance. The prime end of the third period is to get rid of the responsibilities of the worldly life and retiring to a peaceful life of the forest to meditate on the supreme spiritual problems. The last period is the period of complete renunciation of all relations of home and society, country or even the humanity at large. He has no mercy, love or hatred or any feeling for any one. His mind concentrates only on the spiritual freedom or salvation.

After having seen in detail the Varṇa and Āśramadhrma separately, it is essential to have a general view of these two dharmas together. The Varṇāśramadharma in general seems to have a very scientific explanation as described by Dr. Bhagvan Das. He tries to justify this system on scientific grounds. He writes, "This four-fold social organisation was based on a few fundamental, wide-reaching, principles of many sciences, biological, psychological, economic, sociological, educational, dietetic and sexolgical, hygienic and Eugenic"[99] K. V. Rangaswami Aiyangar alsa supports the system of varna and āśrama. He observes: "Indian society was kept from disintegration by the sublime conception of the scheme of varṇa and āśrama, which gave its women and men a clear vision of the spiritual winning post, and showed there how to order their lives and mould their actions in order that they may, in the fulness of time or even in this life itself, triumphantly reach it,"[100]

While discussing the importance of Varṇāśamadharma, we are reminded of Bradley's famous moral dictum of 'My station and its duties.' The duties of an individual follow from the class and stage to which he belongs. Dr. T. M. P. Mahadevan writes; "The duties that are prescribed for the different castes, Varṇa-dharmas as they are called, have for their aim the preservation of society. Each man has his station in the particular social group to which he belongs; and he should perform the duties that pertain to his station."[101]

Bradley's ethical doctrine of 'My station and its duties' is based on the organic view of society. He pleads that man is a social animal and that his sociability is mainly due to the effect of society on him. He observes: "In short, man is a social being; he is real only because be is social and can realise himself because it is as social that he realises himself. The mere individual is a delusion of theory; and the attempt to realise it in practice is the starvation and mutilation of human nature, with total sterility or the production of monstrosities."[102] His doctrine of 'My station and its duties', therefore, attempts to develop the ideal conduct of an individual on the pre-supposition that he is an organ of such an organism. Therefore, every man must feel that his role is determined by his function in that social system and his duties are derived front reflection upon the station or the position that he occupies within it. He says, "To know what a man is (as we have seen) you must not take him in isolation. He is one of a people, he is born in a family, he lives in a certain society, in a certain state. What he has to do depends on what his place is, what his function is, and that all comes from his station in the organism."[103] He further states, "we must content ourselves by pointing out that there are such facts as the family, then in a middle position a man's own profession and society, and, overall, the larger community of the state. Leaving out of sight the question of a society wider than the state, we must say that a man's life with its moral duties is in the main filled up by his station in that system of whole which the state is, and still more by its spirit, gives him the life which he does live and ought to live."[104]

It may not be necessary to go into further details about his theory, but this much is obvious that the ethical doctrine of Bradley resembles the morality expressed in terms of

Varṇāśramadharma in the Hindu ethics. In both the cases, individuals' duties and obligation come from their respective positions and stations in life.

The concept of Varṇāśramadharma is based on the organic theory of society. The ancient Hindu seers introduced the system to keep society stable and to maintain the healthy development of the social organism.

Reference

1. Valavlkar, Pandharinath H, Hindu Social Institutions, P. 281.
2. Maitra, S.K., The Ethics of the Hindus, P.1.
3. Holderness, T. W., Peoples and problems of India, P. 86.
4. Radhakrishnan, S., Eastern Religion and Western Thought, P. 371.
5. Kane, P.V., History of Dharmaśāstra. Vol. II, part I, P. 23.
6. Desai, Mahadev, The Gospel of Selfless Action or the Gītā according to Gandhi, 102-104.
7. Kane, P.V., History of Dharmaśāstra, Vol. II pt. I, P. 54-55
8. Ibid. p. 28
9. Ketkar, S.V., History of caste in India, ed, II; P. XXII
10. Maharaj, Swami., Dharma Theerthaji, The menace of Hindu Imperiatism, p. 23.
11. Nikhilanand, Swami, Hinduism, its meaning for the liberation of the spirit, p. 63.
12. Dutt, Romesh Chandra, The Early Hindu Civilization, p. 57-58.
13. Prasad, Narmadeshwar, The Myth of the Caste-System p. 56.
14. Ibid., p. 60-61.
15. Ghurye, G.S., Caste, Class and Occuration, p. 43.
16. Ibid., p. 43.
17. Radhakrishnan, S. The Hindu view of life, p. 167,
18. Muir, J., Sans. Text, p. 226; Prasad, Narmadeshwar, opp. cit., p. 61.
19. Prasad, Narmadeshwar, The Myth of the Caste System, p. 62.

20. Sastri, K. S. Ramaswami, Studies in Ramayana, p. 99.
21. Bāla, 5, 19.
22. Kiṣk. IV, 6.
23. Sastri, K. S. Ramaswami, Studies in Ramayaṇa, p. 100.
24. Bāla, VI, 17.
25. Dutt, Ramesh Chandra, The Early Hindu Civilization, p. 145.
26. Sen, K. M., Rāmayaṇa, Mahābhārata, And the Puranas, p. 75.
27. Thomas, P., Hindu Religion, Customs and Manners, p. 23.
28. Vora, D. P., The Evolution of Morals in Epics, p. 124.
29. Śānti, 296, 20-21; Cri. edi., 285, 20-21.
30. Ibid, 293, 21.
31. Anu, 141, 68.
32. Ibid, 141, 69.
33. Vana, 180, 21.
34. Ibid, 207m 25.
35. Śānti, 60, 13-14, 189, 5; Udyoga 40, 26.
36. Ibid, 55, 15-16.
37. Droṇas 69, 2.
38. Monier, Williams, Sanskrit Dictionary.
39. Śānti, 60, 21.
40. Śānti, 189, 6.
41. Ibid, 60, 28.
42. Ibid, 203, 1.
43. Renou, Louis, Hinduism, P. 143.
44. Śānti, 189, 7; Cri, edi, 182, 7.
45. Ibid, 60, 30 & 37
46. Ibid, 294, 4
47. Ibid, 63, 12-14.
48. Pandey, Manubhai c., Intelligent Man's Guide to Indian Philosophy p, 265.
49. Valavalkar, Pandarinath H., Hindu social Institutions, p. 327.
50. Śānti, 296m 5-6; Anu, 141, 141, p. 5918 (G.P.), 297, 5-6, (P. C. Roy)

51. Ghurye, G.S., Caste, Class and Occupation, P. 48.
52. Buch, Maganlal A., The Principles of Hindu Ethics, P. 378.
53. Śānti, 181, 5-3; Cri. edi. 188, 5-9.
54. Ibid, 181, 10, Cri. edi. 188, 10.
55. Udyoga, 107, 18.
56. Śānti, 62, 5.
57. Ibid, 63, 4-5.
58. Gītā, IV, 13 (Gītā Rahasya)
59. Śānti, III, 12.
60. Anu, 143, 51 and 26.
61. Vana, 313, 108.
62. Anu, 143, 48-51 and 53; 217, 12-17.
63. Śānti, 296, 28.
64. Vana; 180, 25, Cri. edi. 177.
65. Ibid, 180, 34-34; Cri. edi. 177.
66. Ibid, 180, 31; Cri. edi. 177
67. Ayo, 109, 4. Translated by M. N. Dutt.
68. Narang, Gokul Chand, Real Hinduism, P. 101
69. Sharma, I.C., Ethical Philosophy of India, p. 78.
70. Nesfield, J.C., Brief view of the caste system of the north-west provinces and Oudh, in J.H. Hutton, Caste in India, p. 170
71. Hutton, J.H., Caste in India, p.78.
72. Radhakaishnan, The Hindu View of Life, P. 104.
73. Ibid., p. 167.
74. Dandekar, R. N. The Religion of Man, edited by Morgan, p. 147.
75. Dikshitar, V. R. R., The Concept of Ancient Indian warfare, in the Aryan Path, vol. 17, 1946, p. 63.
76. Thomas, P., Hindu Religion, Customs and Manners, p. 22-23.
77. Mackenzie, John, Hindu Ethics, p. 242.
78. Senart, Emile, Caste in India, the facts and the system, p. 213. Translated by D. Ross.
79. Vaiday, C.V., Epic India, P. 48

80. Tiwari, Brij Gopal, Secularism and Materialism in Modern India, p. 190.
81. Encyclopedia of Religion and Ethics, Art, on Āśrama' by Deussan.
82. Valavalkar, Pandharinath H., Hindu social Institutions, p. 70-71.
83. Śānti, 191, 8.
84. Anu, 141, 36.
85. Śānti, 61, 20.
86. Besant, Annie, Hindu Ideals, p. 28.
87. Anu, 141, 71-73.
88. Śānti 61, 11-12.
89. Śānti, 295, 35.
90. Sharma. I.C., Ethical Philosophy of India p. 79.
91. Anu, 142 13.
92. Śanti, 192, I; 185, 1. Cri. edi.
93. Anu-142, 7-12.
94. Śānti, 61 4.
95. Śānti, 192, 3 Cri, edi 185, 3.
96. Mookerji, Radha Kumud, Ancient Indian Education, P. 326.
97. Radhakrishnan, The Hindu View of Life, p. 91-92.
98. Tiwari, B.G., Secularism and Nationalism in Modern India, p. 190-191.
99. Das, Bhagvan, The Science of social Organisation or the Laws of Manu, Vol. III p. 779.
100. Aiyanger, K. V. Rangaswami, Our social Heritage. P. 39.
101. Mahadevan, T.M.P. The Concept of Dharma in the Mahābhārata, pub. in Vedant Kesari, Vol. 37, p. 20.
102. Bradley, F. H., Ethical Studies, p. 174.
103. Ibid., p. 173.
104. Ibid., p. 174.

3

Political Ethics

The political ethics has been expounded mainly under two heads; viz., 'Rājadharma' and 'Daṇḍanīti.' In the Mahābhārata, they are found mainly in the first two sections of the Śāntiparva entitled, 'the section on duties in times of distress' (Āpaddharma).[1] They are also scattered throughout the epic particularly in Ādiparva, Sabhāparva, Vanaparva, Udyogaparva, Bhīṣmaparva, Anuśāparva and Āśramavaāsikaparva.

Rājadharma and Daṇḍanīti aim at helping people by giving them due protection and justice. In this regard, Bhīśma points out the benefits of the fulfilment of Daṇḍanīti (the science of chastisement) that it forces all men to the observance of the duties of their respective orders. Duty, administered, forces people to virtuous acts[2]. U. N. Ghosal interprets Bhiśma's statement as follow: "Identifying Daṇḍanīti for all practical purposes with Rājdharma, the speaker claims for it a twofold function. Daṇḍaniti, we are told, is the means of ensuring individual security as well as the stability of the social order founded upon the law of its component units."[3]

The rights and duties of both the rulers and the subjects are prescribed in the Daṇḍanītī. The important duties of the kings are ethically significant. The ethical significance of royal office is very high in the epic. According to Indra, casting away life in battle, compassion for all creatures, knowledge of the affairs of the world, protection of men, rescuing them from danger, relieving the distressed and the oppressed, all these occur among the duties practised by the king.[4] The royal duties become prominent when kings are regarded as the makers of age-cycles. In the Śāntiparva, the sage Utathya states that the respective ages called Kṛta, the Tretā, the Dvāpara and the Kaliyuga all are dependent on the conduct of the king. It is the king who constitutes the age.[5] Bhīṣma also subscribes to this view.[6] The paramount importance of the ruler can be understood by visualising the picture of a state of anarchy. The state of anarchy has been analogically illustrated with an example which is called Matsya-Nyāya. i.e., "Like fishes in the water, stronger animals prey on the weaker."[7] Bṛhaspati gives a description of Matsya-Nyāya which prevails necessarily in the absence of royal office. He says to Vasumanā that the duties of all men have their root in the king. It is the king that brings peace on earth, through due observance of duties[8]. If the king does not exercise the duty of protection, the strong will forcibly appropriate the possession of the weak; no body can say this is mine; wife, son, food and other kinds of property will not exist; all persons possessed of wealth will have to encounter death, confinement and persecution; all restrictions about marriage and intercourse will cease; all affairs relating to agriculture and trade will fall into confusion; morality will be lost; the three Vedas will disappear; no marriage will take place; society itself will cease to exist and all kinds of injustice will set in.[5] In the chapters no-90 and 122 of the Śāntiparva, the importance of the royal office for the benefit of both individuals and the community has been highlighted.

The dignity of royal office is, thus very high. The king is given different names according to the different capacities in which he serves the people. The bird Pūjanī says to king Brahmadatta that when the king behaves with compassion towards his subjects, he is called their father. By doing good to the people and by cherishing the poor, the king becomes a mother for his people. By giving instruction in morality and virtue, he becomes a preceptor, and by exercising the duty of protection, he becomes the protector. By scorching the wicked, he comes to be regarded as fire. By rewarding his benefactors with showers of wealth and by fulfilling their ambitions he is called Kubera. By restraining the sinful, he comes to be called Yama.[9]

The popular form of Government in the epic period was monarchy. It was functioning on the pattern of a welfare state, paying attention to the welfare of those who deserve the help and protection from the Government. In the Śāntiparva, Bhīṣma says to Yudhiṣṭhira that he (the king) should always maintain and protect the helpless, the masterless, the old, and women that are widows.[10] Thus the king is under compulsion to uphold the rights and privileges of the helpless people.

Though the form of Government was monarchy, it was limited in exercise of power. The interests of the public were placed above the personal interest. The private sentiments of the royalty were not permitted to stand in the way of the welfare of the public. The king was not at liberty to misuse the national income in the manner he liked. The public interests demanded economy and restricted expenditure of the king. The author of the epic seems to be very careful in this direction. In the Mahābhārata, king Uśīnara states go Gālaba who wants eight hundred horses for 'gurudakṣinā', "My wealth exists only for my subjects residing in the city and the country and not for my own comforts and enjoyment. That king, who gives away for his own pleasure the wealth that belongs to others, can never earn virtue or fame."[11]

In the Rāmāyaṇa also, monarchy or kingship was the form of the Government. K.S. Ramaswami Sastri is of the opinion that the kingship of Vālmīki's age was an limited and constitutional monarchy. It was limited by the powers of the cabinet and the Sabhā on the other hand. If the king disobeyed the Dharmaśāstra and oppressed his subjects, he should be killed, king Vena was thus killed. Sagara banished his eldest son Asamanja.[12] The duties of the king are similar to those described in the Mahābhārata. Daśaratha, in his advice to Rāma on the eve of crowning him as Yuvarāja, says that a king should control impulses born of lust and anger and should know directly the welfare of his subjects and should please his ministers and his people and have full granaries and treasuries and arsenals.[13] In the Rāmāyaṇa, it is pointed out that the king's primary duties are the protection of his subjects from external attack and internal disorder and the rendering of impartial justice. He is a source of righteousness, wealth and desire in the state. He must treat his subjects like his sons.[14]

When we analyse royal duties in general, we find that these different royal obligations are based on the very nature of kingship. Some of the duties of a King follow from the idea of its divine origin. Bhīṣma narrating the old episode of creation of four varṇas out of four organs of the creator indicates that Kṣatriyas are created as the wielder of force to safeguard the people with a view to benefitting them.[15] It is clear that divine purpose is not the only factor behind the creation of four varṇas. However, it is also behind the creation of the King as the necessary factor to rescue the people from evils and from the anarchical state of Nature.[16] Bhīṣma points out that at the time of making Pṛthu the king, the sages and gods instructed Pṛthu to fearlessly accomplish all those tasks in which righteousness resides. They advised him to look upon all creatures with an equal eye, to observe the dictates of righteousness, to punish those who have deviated from the path of duty, to maintain the religion inculcated by the Vedas in thought, word and deed, to fearlessly maintain the duties laid down in the Vedas and to Protect the world from an intermixture of castes.[17] The above said royal obligations are due to the facts accepted as divine origin of the kingship. These duties are assigned to the king by the gods themselves and the ancient Hindu saints and seers. They give these responsibilities to the king, keeping in view the social and individual needs to bring favourable circumstances for the betterment of both society and individuals.

Some of the duties are discharged by the king for rewards or benefits. It is based upon the moral and spiritual grounds of the law of Karma. Bhīṣma observes that only by protecting the subjects, the king earns all religious merits (puṇya) which are acquired by the student's, the householders and the hermits.[18] He also observes that the king goes to heaven in accordance with the measure of his merits or he goes to hell for innumerable years for his commission of sins. In the epic, we find several more verses in its support. For example, in the Śāntiparva, Bhīṣma states that the sin a king incurs by neglecting for a single day to protect his subjects from fear is such that he does not attain in to end of his sufferings (for it) in hell till after a thousand years. The merit a king earns by protecting his subjects righteously for a single day is such that he enjoys its reward in heaven for ten thousand years.[19] Bhīṣma enumerates thirty-six virtues of the king to get blessings on earth and heaven such as, observing duties without wrath and malice and kindness etc.[20] Thus, some of the duties of the king are based on grounds of reward and punishment.

The duties of the king are in the form of the return of the privileges given to him by the people. The royal duties are due to the agreement which the king is supposed to have with his people. The duties he performs in the sense of 'must' are the return for what he receives from his people. The discussion between a bird named Pūjani and king Brahmadatta throws ample light on this contractual nature of royal duties. It is pointed out in the discussion by the bird Pūaji that taking from his subjects a sixth share of their wealth, he (the king) should protect them all. That king who does not protect his subjects is truly a thief.[21] Some of the duties of the king are of contractual nature. The king takes money of the state as his pay for the duties he performs for the benefit of the people. It becomes contractual as it is a matter of 'give and take'. Bhīṣma compares the king with a flowerman and not with a charcoal-maker. The charcoal-maker uproots trees and plants, and burns them for producing his stock-in-trade. The flowerman on the other hand, waters his trees and plants, and gathers only their produce. Thus Bhīṣma states to Yudhiṣṭhira, "Imitate the example O king, of the flowerman and not of the charcoal-maker. Becoming such and discharging the duty of protection, thou mayst be able to enjoy the earth for ever."[22]

Bhīṣma gives a very significant simile to illustrate the royal conduct. The king should always adopt the behaviour of a pregnant women. As the mother, disregarding her own likings, seeks the well-being of the child in her womb, so should the king behave towards his subjects. The righteous king should always behave in a way to give up what is dear to him for the sake of what is beneficial to his people.[23] Really, without the protection from outside, society, as such, ceases to exist. No normal work is possible by the individual, unless he is free to work without any worry or anxiety of self-protection. If protective measures of society are lifted, society, whether civilized or uncivilized would be an impossibility. So, to bring stability in society is the prime royal obligation. And for it, the political organization is necessitated.

The royal duties may be considered under two heads: (i) positive and (ii) negative. Positive duties are those which should be performed by the king as virtues like protection of the people and so on. Negative duties are in the form of prohibitions. In the Śāntiparva, Bhīṣma asks the king to avoid normally eighteen vices, ten proceeding from love of pleasure and eight from anger and loss of temper. The first ten are (i) inordinate passion for hunting, (2) gambling whether with dice or racing, (3) sleeping by day, (4) smutty talk and idle gossip, (5) excessive sexual indulgence, (6) drinking, (7) use of Bhanga, (8) passion for sleeping and singing, (9) dancing and (10) purposeless touring. The other eight are (11) tale hearing (12) philandering, (13) malevolence (14) envy, (15) demeaning oneself, (16) extravagance, (17) foul and harsh speech and (18) inflicting prinishment without justification.[24]

About the positive duties or duties to be performed by the king, Bhīṣma advises the king to observe purity, exertion, truth, vigilance, forbearance, straightforwardness, compassion for all creatures, and steadiness[25]

Ethics of War

War has been justified on several grounds in the epic: ethical, spiritual, social and political grounds. The proposition that fighting battles is the prime royal duty is introduced by Vyāsa in his lesson on Rājadharma to Yudhiṣṭhira "Like a snake which devours a mouse, the Earth devours a king that is inclined to peace and a Brāhmin that is exceedingly attached to a life of domesticity,"[26] Bhīṣma also reiterates that the earth swallows up the king who is averse to battle and the Bhāhmiṇ who is attached to wives and children.[27] There is yet another verse in the epic which very obviously established fighting as the prime duty of the king.[28]

In the epic, we find verses which support fighting on ethical ground. In relation to the ethical basis of fighting, it is stated by Bhṣima in the Śāntiparva: "As the duty of the Brāhmiṇs consists of the practice of charity, study and penances, so the duty of the Kṣatriyas is to cast away their bodies, O Kṛṣna, in battle. A Kṣatriya should slay sires and grandsires, brothers and preceptors and relatives and kinsmen that may engage with him in unjust battle. This is his declared duty."[29] There are other verses too which support fighting battles as the supreme duty of the ruler. In another context, Bhīṣma states, "Death on a bed of repose after ejecting phlegm and urine and uttering piteous cries, is sinful for a Kṣatriya. Surrounded by kinsmen and slaughtering his foes in battle, a Kṣatriya should die at the edge of keen weapons."[30] Thus fighting becomes the moral obligation of the king. If he turns his back from fighting, that will be regarded as an unethical act for that king. Killing or being killed is one of the highest sacrifices. In its support, there is a story of a king named Hayagriva, who after having slain a large number of his foes in battle is himself defeated and slain while without a follower by his side. For doing everything to check foes and to protect people, he acquires great fame from the battles he fought and goes to heaven. Vyāsa says: "Mangled by robbers with weapons, boldly fighting with them and casting off his life in battle, the high-souled Hayagriva, ever attentive to his (kingly) duties, achieved the object of his life and is now enjoying great bliss in heaven."[31]

Fighting is approved on social ground too. The duty of the Kṣatriyas or the king's order to fight is in accordance with the law of their class. It is the class duty. The king is bound to fight not only in reply to a challenge, but also for the suppression of the sinful persons like robbers. Summarizing the duties of the Kṣatrīyas, Bhīṣma says: "Always exerting himself for the destruction of robbers and wicked people he (a Kṣatriya) should put forth his prowess in battle. There is no higher duty for him than the suppression of robbers. Therefore king who desires to acquire religious merit should engage in battle."[32]

Fighting has been justified also on spiritual ground. Fighting has been declared to lead to the reward of spiritual merit and heaven. In the Mahābhārata, the sage king Janaka gives a beautiful account of it showing how Kṣatriyas dying in battle go to heaven and those who return or flee back from battle are tortured in hell.[33] In the chapter No. 99 of the Śāntiparva, Bhīṣma says that he who dies in bettle goes to the place of Indra. And in the chapter No. 98 of the same parva, Indra himself answers the question raised by king Amarīṣa that no one should grieve for the brave who die in the battlefield. They all attain heaven.

In the Rāmāyaṇa too, we find that war has been justified on spiritual ground. It is stated that death in battle leads to heaven. Even a sinful man is purified by his valiant death in battle.[34] In this connection, it should be mentioned here that defensive wars were treated as inevitable and righteous wars were treated as an open doorway to heaven.[35]

Coming to the political ground for fighting, it is enough to say that the existence of kingship depends on it. No one can continue as a king if he is not ready to fight when his authority as a king is challenged. He will have to fight when any rebellion bursts out. Sometimes, in order to bring peace, law and order in the state, fighting becomes necessary.

C. V. Vaidya holds that the motive of battle in the epic age is to establish the superiority of one people over another as when a king was conquered he was made to pay a tribute; if slain, he was replaced by his son or other relatives. In this connection he states, "Though constantly at feud throughout the epic period, there was, however, as has already been shown, no desire, among the states to annihilate one another. There was no desire for the extension of territory by the absorption of neighbouring states, untill we come to about the close of the epic period when political morality declined and when the example of the founding of Persian Empire tempted strong states to imitate it.[36] V.R.R. Dikshitar recognizes religion as the main motive force for fighting battles in ancient India. He does not regard either desire for colonisation or inspiration for conquest as the main cause of fighting. He observes, "Behind their wars and conquests, religion acted as a driving force. It was believed that a soldier who would fight to the finish, who would not retreat on any account, who would die fighting in the field heroically, or who would win over the enemy by valour, reached Virasvarga or heaven. The war was then a means to an end. The goal of every soldier was the attainment of heaven and the sure way of achieving is was to fight and fall heroically in the field."[37] Thus we find that the epic justifies war on the ground that fighting battles is the moral, social, religious and political obligation of the ruler.

It must be mentioned here that in the epic, war is not regarded as an unmixed good. The evil effects of war have also been described by the authors of the epics. There are occasions when war has been regarded as worthless and senseless and has been condemned. The learned speaker Saṁjaya advises Yudhiṣṭhire not to fight with Kauravas.' O Ajātaśatru, if without war, the Kurus will not yield thy share, I think, it is far better for thee to live upon alms in the kingdom of the Andhaka and the Vṛṣṇis than to obtain sovereignty by war."[38] At another place, it is observed that war as a means to achieve any end occupies the last position among the different means. When it becomes necessary to fight for achieving the goal, only then we are permitted to resort to war as a means, otherwise we must employ other means to realise the end. As Vāmadeva says, "First the king should try to conquer with other means than to fight because the things acquired through fighting are regarded as inferior."[39] In the Rāmāyaṇa, offensive war for couquest was regarded as an evil. It is also mentioned that war is the greatest calamity in this sorrowful world and that is afterall an uncertain affair.[40] War is never regarded as one of the aims of life. It should be taken recourse to as the last resort.[41]

Although fighting is opposed sometimes, it is given greater emphasis in the epic. A very important dialogue between a woman named Vidulā and her defeated son Saṁjaya is worth mentioning in this connection. Citing the case of Indra, she presses her son to fight, as a brave man wins fame by slaying even a single foe. She states, "A Kṣatriya, O Saṁjaya, hath been created for battle and victory. Whether he winneth or perisheth, he obtaineth the region of Indra. The happiness that a Kṣatriya obtaineth by reducing his foes to subjection is such that the like of it doth not exist in heaven in the sacred region of Indra."[42] Again Bhīṣma states in Āpaddharma parva: "If he (a king) dies in battle, he goes to heaven and if he wins the battle, he enjoys the kingdom on earth. One who casts off his life in the battle-field, goes to the kingdom of Indra."[43]

These verses emphatically state that in both the cases - whether the result be victory or death - war is morally obligatory on the king. Fighting, as a royal duty, is also given a further incentive by the consideration that by conquering other countries, the king gets name, fame and even religious merits. N. C. Bandyopadhya, holds the same view,[44] Sivaswami Aiyar views territorial aggrandisement or extension of sovereignty as a legitimate ambition in a king.[45]

Thus we find that fighting is regarded as an important royal duty in the epic. The duties pertaining to war may be considered under there heads: viz.,

1. pre-war duties,
2. War-time duties,
3. Post-war duties.

1. Pre-war Royal Duties:

Duties pertaining to pre-war period are both defensive and offensive. The defensive or preparatory duties demand that the king must be careful about the danger from the enemy; he must keep foodgrains in huge stocks, so that in emergency his soldiers may not starve. There should be enough facilities for drinking water. The king must have enough money in his treasury to spend over his soldiers and subjects. Bhīṣma advises Yudhiṣṭira that apart from forts army should vigil over frontiers, towns, parks and pleasure gardens. Spies should be deployed in shops and places of amusements, in meetings and conclaves of the learned, in public places, in his own courts and in the houses of the citizens.[46] He should gather wealth, store oil, fat, honey, clarified butter, medicines, charcoal, fuel and all kinds of weapons.[47] As a defensive measure, the king should set men for destroying the crops on the field of the enemy by creating disunion among the enemy's subjects. Failing to do this, he should destroy those crops by means of his own troops. He should destroy all the bridges in enemy's kingdom and should bale out the water of the tanks and if it is not possible, he should poison the water of the tanks.[48]

Thus the defensive duties are suited to the exigencies of the circumstances. Precautions are taken to avoid the miseries of the people due to war. The requirements of food, house, cloth and even of amusement are met by the king.

The king prepares himself to share all sorts of calamities and sufferings and eventualities falling upon his subjects. When we look at the offensive war duties, we find that even lower means have been sanctioned to overpower the enemy.

Here we may note a shift in the war ethics. It may be said to have declined from early war ethics of the Hindus. Previously, the common innocent people or the workers and peasants were not disturbed in any way by wars. C.V. Vaidya describes the glorious war ethics in this way, "Even the Greeks were struck with admiration at the righteous fighting of the Indians who never disturbed the tiller of the soil not devastated the crops. While fighting is going on the agriculturists securely follow their own occupations; these rules and facts appear in strange contrast with other rules laid down for laying waste the country of the enemy or one's own country to prevent attacks."[49] V.R.R. Dikshitar also regards early Hindu warfare as having no concern with the people. It was only between the states. He observes, 'Curiously, war in ancient India was often between states and not between peoples. One state attacked the other. The people of the state did not participate. It was not a people's war where a whole nation went out in defence of home and hearth. The war was absolutely a matter between two kings."[50] The war in the epic period, on the contrary, appears to affect the common men of the villages. Their crops in the field and water of the tanks are either destroyed or made poisonous for their use.

The king's policy towards his enemies may be called the principle of expediency. The policy should be determined in accordance with the situations in which his enemy is. Bhīṣma advises Yudhiṣṭhira to make peace with those foes with whom (according to the ordinance) peace should be made, and wage war with them with whom war should be waged.[51] He further states that when the king, by a survey of his own, finds himself weak, he should then, in consultation with his counsellors, make peace with a foe that is stronger. The king that is wise should speedily make peace with a foe, even when he knows that he is not weak, if any advantage is to be derived from it.[52] In this connection, Bṛhaspati advises Indra to watch for the lapses of his foes before striking any offensive measures.[53]

Distrust and Treachery as war measures are also recommended. They are accepted as approved principles of royal policy in the epic period. Bharadvāja Kaṇika expresses the need of destroying the enemy to the king Śatruñjaya thus: 'The unpaid balance of a debt, the unquenched remnant of a fire and the unslain remnant of foes, repeatedly grow and increase. Therefore, all these should be completely extinguished and and exterminated."[54] Kaṇika keeping it in his mind that opportunity missed by a man seldom comes again to him, advises Śatruñjaya, thus, "when the occasion comes for intercourse with an enemy, a king possessed of foresight should make peace, without reposing blind truth on him. When the business is over, he should quickly turn away from his new ally. One should conciliate a foe with sweet assurances as if he were a friend. One, however, should always stand in fear of that foe as living in a room within which there is a snake.'[55] There are several more verses which throw light on distrust and treachery being approved as measured to tackle enemies. The King should be gentle in speech and at heart he should be like a razor's edge. In this connection Kaṇika observes: "The person who is desirous of achieving prosperity should join hands, swear, use sweet words, worship by bending down his head, and shed tears. One should bear one's foe on one's shoulders as long as time is unfavourable. When, however, the opportunity has come, one should break him into fragments like an earthen jar on a stone."[56]

These war-tactics were however looked upon as unethical by conscientious thinkers. In the epic, we find very high ranking morality on the one hand and some low standard war ethics on the other. It appears to be quite contrary. It is therefore, worth mentioning in this regard that low level-tactics have not been prescribed in ordinary or general circumstances but they are exclusively meant for the emergent situations. In the Anuśāsanaparva Bhīṣma says to Yudhiṣṭhira, "The ritual sacrifices are the purifiers which purify the kings from the sins and vices which they commit against their enemies for victory,"[57] It is further reiterated by Bhīṣma in the same chapter. It is also held by Vyāsa in chapter No. 71 of the Āśvamedhaparva. A king is permitted to adopt unfair means only when they are indispensably necessary for achieving higher ends. They are sanctioned as the last resort when other means fail and no alternative remains. Vāmadeva states that the ends achieved by peaceful means are superior to those ends achieved by coercion and war.[58]

2. War-time Duties:

In the epic, we find well-recognised ethical canons for ensuring a fair fight or Dharmayuddha. As Sir Gokul Chand Narang observers, "The laws of war laid dawn by Hindu law-givers are most humane."[59] Both the parties follow commonly accepted principles for regulating war-ethics. Some of the rules of war are given thus, "A car warrior should have a car-warrior for his antagonist; he on the neck of an elephant should have a similar combatant for his foe; a horse should be met by a horse, and a foot-soldier, O Bhārata, should be met by a foot-soldier.... Guided by considerations of fitness, willingness, daring and might, one should strike another, giving notice. No one should strike another that is unprepared or panic-struck. One engaged with another, one seeking quarter, one retreating, one whose weapon is rendered unfit, one engaged in mail, should never be struck... Car-drivers, animals (yoked to cars or carrying weapons), men engaged in the transport of weapons, players on drums and blowers of conches should never be struck,"[60] In another context Bhīṣma promulgates his war ethics in this way. "All helpless persons, all persons in sleep, all members of the other sex are unslayable. One that has fallen down, one whose armours has slipped off, one whose standard is down, one who says, 'I am thine, one who bears the name of female, one no longer capable of taking care of one's self, one who has only a single son, or one who is a vulgar fellow, with these, I do not like to battle."[61]

The common principle to be maintained in all warfare is that war must be righteous both in its aim and its method. It should be waged with enemies of equal rank and strength. One essential condition of equitable war is that both the parties must share the same advantage or disadvantage. It is clearly mentioned in the Bhīṣmaparva that persons who are equally circumstanced should encounter each other. Those engaged in contests of words, should be fought against with words. Those that left the ranks should never be slain.[62] Certain other rules and regulations are also observed in the battle. For instance, it is said by Balarāma in chapter No. 60 of the Salyaparva that no limb below the nevel should be struck in fighting with clubs. The use of poisoned and barbed arrows has been disallowed in the battle by Bhīṣma himself in chapter No. 95 of the Śāntiparva.

Thus the battle-field morality in the epic age was of a very high order. It was governed by humanitarian principles. No wounded persons were left to die without proper medical treatment from either side. Bhīṣma in his talk with Yudhiṣṭhīra says, "A wounded opponent should either be sent to his own home, or if brought to the victor's quartes, should have his wound attended to by skillful surgeons."[63]

In the Rāmāyaṇa also, we find that war-ethics was highly developed. The most notable aspect of the righteous war was the non-injury of non-combatants. It will not be out of place to enlist some features of war ethics as found in the Rāmayaṇa. It is considered sinful to kill women, we see that Rāma hesitates to kill Tārakā till a command comes from Viśvāmitra.[64] It is considered improper to begin a war without formal declaration of war.[65] As far as possible, war in the night should be avoided. But sometimes it does take place. It is stated that once during a night-fight Vānaras killed Vānaras and Rākṣasas killed Rākṣasas.[66] It is always observed that non-combatants should not be injured. No third person should interfere while one is fighting with another. When Rāvaṇa is fighting with Nala, hanumana thinks that he should not attack Rāvaṇa at that moment. An enemy when he is drunk or asleep or afraid or unarmed or tired or in the company of women should not be attacked.[67] It is also said that there should be no attack on helpless person or persons who are the only male members in their families or persons who hid themselves or who run away in fear.[68] A high standard of conduct is exhibited by Rāma who finding Rāvaṇa tired, asks him to go home and have rest and come back refreshed wielding a fresh bow and in a fresh chariot.[69]

In spite of such advanced morality of the battle-field, occasional deviations from the normal ethical code are allowed in special circumstances. Bhīṣma advises Duryodhana in the Udyogaparva that deceit must be met with deceit, and crookedness with crookedness. So far as ordinary combatants are concerned, one should fight with them artlessly. As regards those that are possessed of power of deception, one should fight with them with the aways of deception.[70] In extreme crisis, all means are justified for the ultimate end. Kṛṣṇa himself says in the Salyaparva that when the number of one's fees becomes great, then destruction should be effected by contrivances and deceitful means.[71]

Thus there are several occasions when the ethical laws are violated. But those who violate them have to show cause for such violations. This show-cause system indicates that without justified grounds no one is permitted to violate these principles. For example, violating one of such principles. Bhīma killed Duryodhana by hitting him in the thigh. After protests from Balarāma, Kṛṣṇa explains why Bhīmā was forced to violate the code. First, Bhīma had to keep his promise to kill him: secondly, it was the curse of saint Maitreya, thirdly, Abhimanyu was killed by violating the code and fourthy, Duryodhana had insulted Draupadī by inviting her to sit on his lap and unclothed his thigh for the purpose, which required such appropriate punishment.[72] Similarly, Kṛṣṇa also affords a justification for Arjuna's killing for Karṇa, when the latter was unarmed to raise his (Karṇa's) chariot's wheel sunk into the ground. Kṛṣṇa justifies it on the ground that similar unrighteous deeds of Karṇa were responsible for it. He meets his death as a punishment.[73] Thus we find that it was morally approved to adopt severe measures against evil-doors. To meet unrighteous and unfair men and to annihilate them, the epic permits violation of warfare ethics and the use of unfair means.

In normal cases, however, the Mahābhārata stresses the maintenance of warfare-ethics. It enjoins compassion for the wounded soldiers and prohibits the use of poisonous weapons. Thus the warfare morality in the epic is based on humanitarian principles.

3. Post-war Royal Duties:

The epic also lays down post-war ethical principles. After war the victorious king should not disturb the law and order of that state. To maintain political stability, he should try to enthrone the nearest relative of the former fuler of the conquered kingdom. It is essential that after the conquest he should treat the subjects of the kingdom as his own. He should pay proper attention towards them and he must try to do maximum good to them as if they were his own subjects. Bhīṣma in the Śāntiparva observes, "It is true, kings desirous of victory afflict many creatures, but after victory they advance and aggrandise all."[74] Doing good to the people of that land, the victorious king purifies his sins of killing people. The foremost duty of the victorious king towards the people is to please them by good speeches and gifts. The excitable classes of a kingdom recently conquered should, without delay, be conciliated with soothing speeches and gifts. This is the good policy for the king to adopt.[75] It is essential to please the people of the conquered country. If these people are not pleased they will become envious and there is every possibility of their betrayal and they may try to dethrone him. So, both for his own safety as well as for righteous purpose, the victorious king should try to please the citizens of the conquered country. The king ought to forgive his enemies. In this connection, the advice of Bhīṣma to Arjuna is noteworthy. He says, "The fame of a king who displays forgiveness after conquest spreads more widely. The very foes of a person that is of a forgiving disposition trust him even when he becomes guilty of a grave transgression. Sambarasura has said that having afflicted a foe first, forgiveness should be shown afterwards, for a wooden pole, if made straight without the application of heat in the first instance very soon assumes its former state."[76]

Thus the royal duties after war are to pacify the tension and to make the rule stable and popular. The king should discharge his royal duties in such a way that the conquered people may regard him as their own king and may get due benefits from him.

Inter-State Morality:

In the epic period, there were small states in India which were often at feud and employed all kinds of means for conquest. V.V. Dixit, quoting Kaṇika nīti says, "Kaṇikanīti contains a synopsis of the policy to be followed by a state (king) towards its rivals. It is frankly unscrupulous."[77] To him, "In fact international morality was very low as it had been even for ages all over the world."[78] No doubt Kaṇikanīti gives a picture of unscrupulous enter-state policy but on the bases of such policies no general conclusions should be drawn. Kaṇika, the propounder of such unscrupulous policies, stands for materialistic and egoistic ethical philosophy in the epic. Naturally all his advocacies are predominantly materialistic, egoistic and sub-standard in tone in comparison to the general ethics of the peic era. Apart from the occasional feuds among the states at intervals, the states are found to live peacefully together sharing the prosperity and calamities. No doubt all small kingdoms are under the overlordship of one big powerful kingdown but this does not mean bitter relations among themselves as there is no regular interference from big states. Mutual good-will, co-operation and mutual understanding appear to form the basis of the inter state morality. In this connection, C. V. Vaidya observes, "The

Indian Aryans had come to lay down rules of fighting which can stand in comparison with modern international law. The Mahābhārata was the beginning of the decline of this high morality of the sword and by the end of the epic period it had deplorably deteriorated."[79]

Duties of the subject:

The duties of the subject follow from the very nature of the contract which was entered into by the people on the one hand and the ruler on the other. Bhīṣma says that people agree to give Manu fiftieth part o their animals and a tenth part of their grains, maidens to him in marriage. Those persons who are trained in using weapons, driving vehicles, and riding animals will follows him like the deities behind Indra. A fourth part of the merit which men will earn under his protection will be his.[80]

Subjects owe to their kings the holy duty of loyalty and obedience. Any injury to royal prestige or interest in highly condemned as the king is regarded as a God by his people. Bṛhaspati speaks to Vasumanā in this connection, "No one should disregard the king by taking him for a man, for he is really a high divinity in human form."[81]

People's Assembly

The assemblies of the people are not ineffective in the epic period. People enjoy both civil and constitutional freedom even in participation in the matters of the kingdom. People share considerably both in the election and the dismissal of a king. However, it is the custom and tradition that the oldest son should succeed the king but the saint as well as people of the country and the ministers have powers to make a noble and able man a king. In the Śāntiparva, it is stated by Bhīṣma that when the king Vena was unable to rule he was killed by the people and the saints, and afterwards his son Pṛthu was enthroned as the ruler of the people.[82] In the Śāntiparva, we find verses authorising the subjects to slay a king if required. The epic enjoins, "That king who tells his people that he is their protector, but who does not or is unable to protect them, should be slain by the combined subject, like a dog that is affected by the rabies and has become mad."[83]

It must be made clear, however, that in practice people were not so free in choosing or dismissing a king. Their right to do so was very much limited and restricted. If the people had unlimited powers the Pāṇḍavas would not have been driven out of the kingdom. But we find that the people kept silent when Yudhiṣṭhira lost his kingdom and was banished for thirteen years.

But there are other occasions when people participate in other political matters. After fifteen years of the Kurukṣetra war, the king Dhṛtarāṣṭra who grows very old, wants to retire to the forest life. He asks Yudhiṣṭhira to summon the people. He meets the Paura Janapadas, Brāhmiṇ and dependent kings. He addresses them and asks them to give him permission. In the beginning the people are found very much moved, but in the end they give him permission to retire to the forest.[84] It is evident from this fact that public opinion was not ignored by rulers. The people had some say in the royal succession.[85] In a discourse between Yudhiṣṭhira and Bhīṣma concerning the different duties of the subject, Bhīṣma holds the coronation of the king as the first duty of the subject. He says: "the coronation of a king is the first duty of a kingdom. A kingdom in which anarchy prevails becomes weak and is soon afflicted by robbers."[86]

Presenting gifts to the king and to honour him are important it duties of the subject. We are told in the epic by Bhīṣma: "One that is honoured by his own people becomes an object of regard with his foes also, while one that is disregarded by his own is overridden by foes. If the king is overridden by his foes, all his subjects become unhappy. Therefore umbrellas, vehicles and outward ornaments, and viands, and drinks, and mansions, and seats, and beds, and all utensils for use and show, should be assigned to the king."[87] We are further told that in return for such offering and gifts the king must discharge his different duties towards his people. He gets all his requirements fulfilled by his subjects so that he may not waste his time in the fulfilling of his own needs. He devotes ample time to the service of the people. At the time of calamities and troubles subjects must sacrifice their petty interests and serve the ruler. They should not hesitate to give high taxes in enriching the royal treasury. Bhīṣma describes the duties of the state and individuals in this way, "The king and the kingdom should always mutually protect each other. This is an eternal duty. As the king protects, by spending all his possessions, the kingdom when it sinks into distress, even so should the kingdom protect the king when he sinks into distress."[88]

The people must respect the king and bow their heads before him. In the words of Bhīṣma, "Like disciples humbling themselves in the presence of the preceptors as the gods in the presence of Indra, all men should humble themselves before the king."[89] Bṛhaspati advises the subject not to touch the belongings of the king as one who appropriates the wealth of the king meets with destruction and sinks into a deep hell of eternal gloom and infamy. Hence an intelligent person should always protect the property of the king as his own and should always be attached to the king.[90] Even to think of doing harm to the king is regarded as morally bad. To quote Bṛhaspati, "That man who even thinks of doing an injury to the king, without doubt meets with grief here and goes to hell hereafter."[91]

In short, attitude of subjects towards their ruler was that of reverence, loyalty, obedience and sacrifice. The ideal relation between the ruler and the ruled consisted in mutual confidence and co-operation. The office of the king was looked upon as divine. So the king had to justify the faith reposed in him by serving the people as best as he could.

Reference

1. Śānti, chap. 56-178; 56-167 Cri, edi.
2. Ibid, 69, 76.
3. Ghosal, U.N, A history of Indian political Idea, p. 193.
4. Śānti, 64, 27.
5. Ibid, 91, 6.
6. Ibid, 69, 80-81
7. Ibid, 15, 30.
8. Ibid, 68, 8-22.
9. Śānti, 139, 103-106; 137, 99-102 Cri. edi.
10. Ibid, 86, 24.
11. Udyoga, 118, 13-14.
12. Sastṛi, K.S. Ramaswami, Studies in Rāmāyaṇa, p. 106.
13. Ayodhyā, III, 41-45.
14. Araṇyaka, Vi, 11-12, 14; L, 9 Uttars L. XXIV, 30-31.
15. Śānti, 72, 4, 5 and 7.
16. Ibid, 59, 14-28.
17. Ibid, 59, 103-108.
18. Ibid, 71, 30.
19. Ibid, 71, 28-29.
20. Ibid, 70, 3-13.
21. Śānti, 137, 96; Cri. edi, 139, 109.
22. Ibid, 71, 20.
23. Ibid, 56, 45-46.
24. Śānti, 56, 42, (Footnote, 9. 4563. G.P.)
25. Ibid, 120, 5.
26. Ibid, 23, 15.

27. Ibid, 57, 3.
28. Udyoga, 134, 11.
29. Śānti, 55, 14-15.
30. Ibid, 97; 23, 28.
31. Ibid, 24, 34-26
32. Śānti, 60, 14, 17 & 18.
33. Ibid, 99, 4-5
34. Yuddha, XLi, 69.
35. Ayodhyā, Lxiv, 41, 42.
36. Vaidya, C. V. Epic India, p. 245.
37. Dikshitar, V. R. R., The Concept of Ancient Indian Warfare, Published in The Aryan Path, Vol, 17th, 1946. p. 64.
38. Udyoga, 27, 1-2.
39. Śānti, 94, 1-2.
40. Sund., XXVII, 53.
41. Yuddha, IX, 8.
42. Udyoga, 135, 11-14.
43. Śānti, 129, 12 Cri, edi.; 131, 12.
44. Bandyopadhya, Narayan Chandra, Development of Hindu Polity & Political Theories, p. 166-167.
45. Aiyar, Sivaswami, Evolution of Hindu Moral Ideal, p. 114
46. Śānti, 69, 7, 12-13.
47. Ibid, 68, 51, 66-57
48. Ibid, 69, 38-39.
49. Vaidya, C. V., Epic India, dp. 261-262
50. Dikshitar V. R. R., The Concept of Ancient Indian Warfare, Pub. in the 'Aryan Prth', Vol, 17th, 1946, p. 64.'
51. Śānti, 57, 4.
52. Śānti, 69, 12, 19-20.
53. Ibid, 103, 17 to 23.
54. Ibid, 138, 58, and 61 Cri. Edi.; 140, 58 to 61.
55. Ibid, 138, 14-15, Cri. edi; 140, 14-15.
56. Ibid, 138, 17-18, Cri. edi; 140, 17-18.

57. Anuśā, 61, 4.
58. Śānti 94, 1.
59. Narang, Gokul Chand, Real Hinduism, p. 163.
60. Bhīṣma, 1, 27-30 & 32.
61. Ibid, 107, 77-79.
62. Ibid, I, 28.
63. Śānti, 95, 13.
64. Bāla, XXVI, 18.
65. Araṇya, XXXVI, 7.
66. Ayodhyā, LV, 22.
67. Kiṣk, LV, 22.
68. Bāla, v, 20.
69. Ayodhyā, LIX, 144.
70. Udyoga, 193, 10.
71. Salya, 61, 67.
72. Ibid, 60, 16-18 & p. 4302-4303, G.P.
73. Karṇa, 91, 6-11.
74. Śānti, 97, 4.
75. Ibid, 96, 12.
76. Ibid, 102, 29-31.
77. Dixit, V. V., Relation of the Epics to the Brāhmaṇ Literature, p. 16.
78. Ibid, p. 17.
79. Vaidya, C.V., Epic India, P. 246.
80. Śānti, 67, 23-24, 29.
81. Ibid, 68, 40.
82. Ibid, 59, 44-110.
83. Anuśā, 61, 32-33.
84. Āśrama, Chap. 8 & 9
85. Dasgupta, Rama Prasad, A Study in Hindu and European Political System, p. 241.
86. Śānti, 67, 2.
87. Ibid, 67, 36-37.

88. Śānti, 130, 30-31
89. Ibid, 67, 34.
90. Ibid, 68, 51-55.
91. Ibid,68, 39.

4

The Problem of Fate and Free Will

In the Hindu ethics, the emphasis is laid upon human efforts or human endeavours. The Bhagvadgītā, which is the soul of the Hindu ethics advocates the essentiality of activism. In this connection M. Hiriyanna observes, "This important element in the conception of the poem would lose its entire significance if we did not regard action as its essential lesson. We may accordingly conclude that the central point of the teaching is activism, or, to use the expression of the Gītā, Karma-yoga."[1] At another place, he remarks, "The point to which it is necessary to draw special attention in this connection is that the Gītā requires man to continue to work even in this perfected state, there being nothing in outer activity which is incompatible with inner peace. Here we see the exalted position assigned to work by the Gītā. It contemplates no period, when activity may be wholly renounced. Passivity, in its view, is almost as reprehensible as wrong activity."[2] Passivism is not allowed even in the state of emancipation. We may think of avoiding actions but really it is an impossibility to avoid them altogether in our life. Without performing action we cannot exist. Though we may try yet, none can refrain from performing physical activities while still living. Life is another name for action and death for inaction. To, Dr. C.D. Sharma "The Gītā tries to build up a philosophy of Karma based on Jñāna and supported by Bhakti in a beautiful manner."[3]

Very often a question is asked whether a man is free to perform his work or he is only a helpless agent in the hands of his Fate. In other words, whether his actions are pre-determined or determined by his own will, this question is discussed elaborately also in the great epic.

From early times, there has been a tendency to recognise an authority other than human being which not only controls our thought but also determines our actions. This power is known as Fate or Destiny. Sometimes the gods are regarded responsible for our actions because they are supposed to shape human Destiny. In the Sabhāparva, Saṁjaya says to Dhṛtarāṣṭra, "The gods first deprive that man of his reason unto whom they send defeat and disgrace. It is for this that such a person seeth things in a strange light. When destruction is at hand, evil appeareth as good unto the understanding polluted by sin, and the man adhered to it firmly. That which is improper appeareth as proper, and that which is proper appeareth as im-proper unto the man about to the overwhelmed by destruction, and evil and impropriety are what he liketh."[4] Further, Kāla or Time is given the same status as that of Destiny to influence human affairs by Saṁjaya in the same context.

Thus Time or Destiny shows its capacity to influence human affairs by influencing the thinking capacity of the individual which dictates human actions. The operations of Fate are regarded as unavoidable as old age and death. The role of Destiny in life is sure to come and cannot leave life unaffected by itself. All beings are alike subject to its sway. It is one of the deepest convictions of men.

The extreme influence of Destiny is marked in the Udyogaparva. King Dhṛtarāṣṭra is regarded as a staunch supporter of this fatalism. He observes about Destiny thus, "I regard Destiny to be superior, and Exertion useless, for although I understand the evil consequences of war that will lead only to ruin, still I am unable to restrain my son who rejoices in gambling and considers his deceit to be wisdom. Understanding everything, I am not yet able to secure my own welfare."[5] In the same chapter, saṁjaya illustrates three factors which determine our action and destiny is one of them. He says, "In the respect three points are entertained; some say that everything is ordained by God; some say that our acts are the result of free-will; and others say that our acts are the result of those of our past lives."[6] In the Śāntiparva the sage Vyāsa says to Śukadeva that the reasons which complment to acts, are three fold. He says, "With respect to acts, some men say that Exertion (human effort) is their cause. Others say that Necessity (Destiny) is their cause. Others again maintain that Nature is the cause."[7] On another occasion he regards these reasons as fourfold. A person is driven to action by four agencies; they are, God, the individual himself (Puruṣa), inherent nature and Destiny-fruits of the past actions."[8] He analyses these factors to show that the real cause of the great war is the will of God. War was pre-ordained. So, Yudhiṣṭhira is not responsible for the killing of relatives and preceptors.

It is observed more than once in the epic that a person is only an instrument in the hands of Destiny. In the Vanaparva, there is a long passage supporting Destiny and absolute dependence upon God. "An old history", says Draupadī, "is cited as an illustration for the truth that men are subject to the will of God and never to their own wishes... O hero amongst men, as a wooded doll is made to move its limbs by the wire-puller, so are creatures made to work by the lore of all ... Every one is subject to God and none else. No one can be his own ordainer... Like light straws dependent on strong winds, all creatures, O Bhārata are dependent on God"[9]:

Absolute dependence upon God is also stressed at several places in the Śāntiparva Aśura Namuuci believing in the control of God over human beings, states, "There is one ordainer and no second. His control extends over the being that lies within the womb... One gets those things that are ordained to be got. That which is to happen actually happens. One has repeatedly to reside in wombs in which one is placed by the ordainer. One has no choice in the matter."[10]

A discussion between Indra and an Asura King named Bali is worth mentioning in this connection. Bali realizes in his life that man does nothing independently but in accordance with the well of God. He says, "When one slays another, one slays only that other's body. That man, who thinks that it is he who slays another, is himself slain. Indeed, both of them are ignorant of the truth viz., he who slays and he who is slain. That person, O Maghavan, who having killed or vanquished any one brags of his manliness, should know that he is not the actor but the act (of which he boasts) has been accomplished by a real agent (who is different)."[11] Bali very firmly asserts the superiority of Kāla or Time in his discussion. Time, to him, is the most powerful thing in the universe, He states, "It is Time that ordains all things. Do not O Śakra, brag of thy manliness.'[12] In the same chapter he describes several times in several manners about 'Kāla'. He goes to such an extent that he regards Time as Brahman. In this connections he states, "Brahman in the form of Time is the refuge of all creatures. Where wouldest thou go transcending that Time? Time of Brahman, indeed, cannot be avoided by running nor by staying still. All the five senses are incapable of perceiving Brahman."[13]

Vyāsa also admits the omnipotence of Kāla or Time, which dictates all human affairs. He says, "Without doubt Time assumes diverse shapes. It has neither beginning nor end. It is Time which produces all creatures and again devours them. I have already spoken of it to thee. Time is the origin of all creatures. Time is that which makes them grow. Time is that which is their destroyer; and lastly it is Time that is their ruler."[14] While explaining the cause of war to Yudhiṣṭtira,

Vyāsaaccepts Time as its only cause. He causes creatures to be slain through the instrumentality of creatures. He compares human beings with the instrument which are being used by the will of the users. So also the entire universe is controlled by Time.[15]

In the Maṇkigītā, Destiny is treated as the supreme entity. Maṇki says, if wealth be not ordained by Destiny, it can never be acquired by even a clever man exerting himself with attention and confidence and accomplishing with skill all that is necessary towards that end. I had, before this, endeavoured by diverse means and devotion to earn wealth. Behold this misfortune brought about by Destiny to the property I had?"[16]

On another occasion Dhṛtarāṣṭa again argues in favour of Destiny, "Man is not the disposer of either his prosperity or adversity. He is like a wooden doll moved by strings. Indeed the Creator hath made man subject to Destiny."[17] Dhṛtarāṣṭra shows his helplessness before pre-destined things to Vidura who teaches him to do good for both his own self and his sons as well as for the Pāṇḍavas. He realises his helplessness thus, "Although, however, I incline in my mind towards the Pāṇḍavas even as thou tea chest me to do, yet as soon as I come in contact with Duryodhana it turneth off in a different way. No creature is able to avert Fate. Indeed Destiny, I think, is certain to take its course; individual exertion is futile."[18]

Yudhisṭira also tries to establish the superiority of Destiny over human endeavour in the Anuśāsanaparva. He says, "It is seen that if a person happens to be unfortunate, he fails to acquire wealth, how soever his strength. On the other hand, if one happens to be fortunate, he comes to the possession of wealth, even if he be a weakling or a fool."[19] He further remarks, "If wealth were the result of exertion then one could, with exertion, acquire it immediately.... Among men, that which is not (destined) to be attained, O chief of the Brāratas is never attained."[20] He cites many other examples in this connection.

The belief in Destiny was widespread among princess, kings, saints, seers and common people. When Dhṛtatāṣṭra was seeking permission from his subjects for going out of the kingdom for Vānaprasthya, a Brāhmiṇ speaking on behalf of subjects points out that Destiny is supreme and cannot be resisted. He maintains. "The destruction that has overtaken the Kurus was not brought about by Duryodhana. It was not brought about by thee. Nor was it brought about by Karṇa and Subala's son. We know that it was brought by Destiny, and that it was incapable of being resisted by human exertion."[21]

This fatalism or determinism was deep-rooted among people in the epic age. Leading persons like king Dhṛtarāṣṭra and Vyāsa had firm faith in the mighty power of Destiny over human affairs. In the above illustrations, Fate appears to be taken as a super-human force, which guides the destinies of men.

But there are persons in the epic who are opposed to this fatalism and believe in the potency of human efforts. To them, human effort is only means in achieving any goal and each and everything depends upon action and Exertion for its existence. If Destiny is accepted there is no meaning in performing actions. Basudeo Saran Agrawal rightly remarks after defining fatalism that fatalism accepts every minute of past, present and future and every action of human life as fixed and predetermined and that there is no scope for performing action voluntarily or rationally by human being.[22] At another place, he maintains that king Dhṛtarāṣṭra and Yayāti were the supporters of fatalism while Vidura and Kṛṣaṇ were the supporters of Rationalism or Prajñāvāda.[23]

In the Mahābhārata, there are verses which decisively establish the potency of human efforts and negate the existence of Fate or Destiny. In the Parāśaragītā, we find a sceptic, argument negating the existence of Fate. It runs thus: "I do not behold that anything in this world is the result of Destiny or the virtuous and sinful acts of Past lives. Inference cannot establish the existence or operation of Destiny.'[24] In the Udyogaparva Kṛṣṇa speaks to Saṁjaya of the superiority of Karma over all other things by pointing out that all things depend on Karma and nothing else. He says "A thirsty person drinks water, and by this act his thirst is allayed. This result proceeds no doubt, from work. There in lies the efficacy of work. If any one thinks that something else is better than work, I deem him weak, and his words are meaningless."[25] The Karma does not influence the world of ours alone, but the world of gods and the objects of nature also. Gods are supposed to reach the state of perfection only due to their Karma.

According to Kṛṣṇa, it is due to work that gods flourish, wind blows, sun rises everyday, fire burns, earth sustains this great burden and the rives carry water satisfying all beings. Kṛṣṇa gives a number of examples to indicate that persons have gone to higher status due to their virtuous conduct, such as Indra, Bṛhaspati, the Rudras, the Adityas, the Vasus, King Yama and Kuvera etc.[26] Bhīṣma himself accepts Exertion as superior to Fate. He advises Yudhiṣṭhira to do his duties because only human efforts are important and not Fate. He says, "O son, thou shouldest always exert with promptitude, O Yudhiṣṭhira, for without promptitude of Exertion mere Destiny never accomplishes the objects cherished by kings. These two, viz., Exertion and Destiny, are equal (in their operations). Of them, I regard Exertion to be superior, for Destiny is ascertained from the results of what is begun with Exertion."[27]

Brahmā, when asked by Vasiṣṭha as to which among these two - Destiny and Exertion, is the more potent in shaping his life, holds the superiority of Karma over Destiny. He takes one's act as soil and his destiny as seed. Seed cannot grow without soil. Similarly, Destiny will not work at all. All good and bad, right and wrong, pain and pleasure come when actions are done. Heaven cannot be attained without Exertion. Destiny is incapable of any effect without human efforts. One cannot live without work.[28] What to talk of human being, even the Supreme Lord Viṣṇu has to perform actions, compulsorily. Bramhā adds, "Even He, the adorable Viṣṇu, who created the three worlds with the Daityas and all the gods, even He is engaged in austere penaces in the bosom of the deep."[29]

Karma produces its fruit and influences the Destiny of man. To prove this fact, Brahmā cites a number of cases. The cases of Yayāti, Aśvatthāmā, Bali (Asura), Nṛga and that of Pāṇḍavas are important.[30] In this connection he concludes his long saying thus, "The man that does not exert himself is never contented in this world nor can Destiny after the course of a man that has gone wrong. So there is no authority inherent in Destiny. As the pupil follows his own individual preceptor, so Destiny follows Exertion."[31]

In the Vanaparva, Draupadī inspires Yudhiṣṭhira to work for the regaining of the kingdom showing the supremacy of human efforts over human Destiny. She advises him to perform actions even if they do not give results. That man is worthless who believes in Chance and Fate. Fatalism makes a man idle and inactive. So, efforts should not be abandoned. She says, "If a creature acteth not, its course of life is impossible. In the case of a creature, therefore, there must be action and not inaction. Thou also shouldest act, and not incur censure by abandoning action.... He that lieth at ease, without activity believing in Destiny, along, is soon destroyed like an unburnt earthen pot in water, so also he that believeth in Chance, i.e., sitteth inactive, though capable of activity, liveth not long, for his life is one of weakness and helplesshess."[32] Miseries and calamities, pain and suffering , diseases of all sorts are due to deeds and hence may be eliminated by fresh efforts.

Thus there are verses in the epic which support both Destiny and human Efforts. Generally speaking, persons like, Vidura, Kṛṣṇa, Bhīṣma and Draupadī emphasise the value of human efforts, while Dhṛtarāṣṭra and Yudhiṣṭhira stress the importance of Destiny. Bhīṣma observes, "Daiva and Puruṣārtha are equally important like the two wheels of a chariot, yet I consider puruāṣṛtha to be better of the two, because its result can be seen in this life while Fate is decided in the next."[33]

It can be said both Destiny and Exertion, are necessary in bringing about the final fruit. Success is the result of the co-operation of many causes. In the Anuśāsanaparva Brahmā says, "Destiny does not help the man that is steeped in spiritual ignorance and avarice. Even as a fire of small proportion, when fanned by the wind, becomes of mighty power, so does Destiny, when joined with individual Exertion, increase greatly (in potentiality)."[34] He says, "By the influence of Destiny, and by putting forth individual Exertion, do men attain to heaven. The combined aid of Destiny and Exertion, becomes efficacious."[35]

In the Rāmāyaṇa also, we find a firm conviction in Fate. After the death of Vālī, Sugriva has a strong fit of remorse and grief. Rama pacifies him by saying that they are controlled by Fate.[36] It has also been maintained that we can over-come Fate by our Efforts.[37] But the best course is to harmonize Fate and Effort. Hence, it is stated that when Fate and Effort combine; the result are rapid and easy and quickly attained. But if and when they conflict, human effort can conquer, or at least modify, the power of Fate.[38]

It cannot be doubted that a man controls his own actions to a great extent. However, he cannot be sure and confident of the success of his actions. It is simply because success depends on several grounds and circumstances. No doubt, some of these circumstances are beyond one's control and some are under his control. Human effort is accepted as one of the important factors in the final outcome but not the only factor. Draupadī says in the Vanaparva. "How can one know beforehand what the consequences will be? Having exerted thyself, thou wilt known the fruit of thy exertions will be. The tiller tilleth the soil with the plough, and soweth the seeds therein. He then sitteth silent, for the clouds (after that) are cause that would help the seeds to grow into plants. If, however, the clouds favour him not, the tiller is absolved from all blame. Whether it be success of failure there should be no despair, for success in acts dependeth upon the union of many circumstances."[39]

One would hardly deny that had all results been dependent on efforts all human desires and wishes would be fullfilled. We have to believe in something other than efforts, which decides the results of the actions performed by men and that is the Destiny of man. But for all practical purposes, it should be accepted that man is the master of his own actions and hence responsible for them. The bird Pūjanī takes Destiny and Exertion as interdependent on each other.[40]

Sushil Kumar De commenting on this problem in the epic writes, "The epic accepts all the implications of the inexorable Karma doctrine and believes in the fatality of human acts as much as it believes in fate itself as divinely ordained. But it also asserts that fate is 'for eunuchs'; and that the fruits of action can be modified by the effort.'[41] Maganlal A. Buch also observes thus; 'The power of Karma or human agency is equally emphasised as fate or destiny. Effort is no negligible factor in the constitution of the universe. It is equally fundamental."[42] He gives equal importance to both Karma and Fate, but the former is the root of the latter. In this connection D. P. Vora states; "In all such discussions, even though the power of fate over human efforts is accepted and it is declared that in spite of a well guarded course of action in the life, a person may have to face disaster because of some actions committed in his previous life, yet it presents us with a dynamic view of life according to which a person can fight against destiny and try for a better fate for putting forth efforts."[43]

In the Anuśāsanaparva, there is a discussion relating to the potency of human. Efforts initiated, on the death of the boy who dies by snake-bite, to know the real cause of his premature death. The discussion very logically and systematically leads us to the conclusion that the death is not due to his Fate but owing to his own deeds. The conversation takes place among Death, Gautami, Kāla, the Fowler and the Serpent. The Fowler named Arjunaka blames the Serpent for this death and hence he wants to kill the Serpent. Gautami, the mother of the boy, thinks that Destiny is its cause, while the fowler thinks the Serpent as the immediate cause. Gautami requests him, "Do thou O Arjunaka of little understanding, release this Serpent. It does not deserve death at thy hands. Who is so foolish as to disregard the inevitable lot that awaits him and burdening himself with such folly sinks into sin?"[44] The Serpent defends himself on the ground that he is bound by Death. He is an instrument. He says. "O foolish Arjunaka, what fault is there of mine? I have no will of my own, and am not independent. Mṛtyu (Death) sent me on this errand. By his direction have I bitten this child, and not out of any anger or choice on my part. Therefore, if there be any sin in this, O Fowler, the sin is his,"[45] However, the fowler is not convinced and takes the Serpent as instrumental cause and thinks him responsible for the death. He thus remark, "If thou hast done this evil, led there to by another, the sin is thine also as thou art an instrument in the act. As in the making of an earthen vassal the potter's wheel and rod and other things are all regarded as causes, so art thou, O Serpent, (cause in the production of this effect)."[46]

The fowler raises a very important ethical issue by putting a question: If whatever is done is pre-determined and fixed then, what is the use of ethics at all? No work is good or bad in itself. The fowler says to the Serpent that if a doer is not at fault for doing a bad work according to you, then why are the thieves and murderers killed or punished for their crimes by the king? Then they should not be blamed for their crimes.[47]

Here the point at issue is: whether man is free or not in his actions. If a man is not free in his actions then to pass moral judgements regarding his actions is meaningless, useless and thus superfluous. If the proposition that man is not free - is true, then the whole science of ethics is untrue. Moral judgement presupposes freedom of will. Non-voluntary actions are not the subject-matter of ethics.

The discussion in the story still goes ahead. Mṛtyu (Death) having been blamed for the death by the Serpent defends himself, "Guided by Kāla, I, O Serpent, sent thee on this errand and neither art thou nor am I the cause of this child's death... The whole universe, O Serpent, is imbued with this same influence of Kāla... Knowing this, why dost thou, O Serpent, consider me to be guilty? If any fault is attached to me in this, thou also wouldst be to blame."[48] Being blamed for the death of the boy, Kāla (Fate) himself appears to defend his case by blaming the previous actions of the boy himself responsible and none else. He says, "Neither Mṛtyu (Death) nor this Serpent, nor am I, O Fowler, guilty of the death of any creature. We are merely the immediate, exciting causes of the event. O Arjunaka, the Karma of this child formed the exciting cause of our action in this matter. There was no other cause of his death. It was killed as a result of its own karma (action). It has met with death as the result of its action in the past. Therefore, neither art thou, nor am I, nor Mṛtyu, nor the Serpent, nor the old Brāhmiṇ lady, is the cause of this child's death. He himself is the cause here."[49]

We have referred to the whole discussion in detail, because it answers the question raised above. This intellectual discourse implies in the first place that Destiny is nothing but the past deeds of Karmas of the individual which influence his future and present behaviour. In other words, Fate is the name of stored results of human deeds in the past which are responsible for our present actions. Secondly, the law of Karma is the law of causation in the field of morality. Thirdly, human being s are responsible for their actions. Men are responsible only when they are free to act. So, this responsibility implies freedom of will.

Sometimes it is felt that some outside entity influences human deeds. It is nothing but past deeds showing their consequences on the doer at that time. The ghost of Destiny is nothing but the consequences stored of his previous Karmas (deeds) in this life or in the other. So it is the man himself and his deeds which are the subject of ethics and in its turn the ethics remains useful and meaningful. So, the human endeavour or his karma is the supreme agency and not the Fate. G. A. Chandavarkar also regards Fate as the consequences of previous deeds. He writes, "There is nothing like fate. Fate means nothing more than the result of the actions done in the past birth."[50] Pandharinath Valavalkar also detines Fate in the same way. "Destiny or Fate is not a mere accident or chance of happening in our life. It is due to the past karma. It is the effect of past karma."[51] E. W. Hopkins regards Fate as the implication of Karma doctrine.[52]

The notion of Fate is dependent upon the concept of law of Karma which is working everywhere. It simply means that all actions good or bad, produce necessarily their proper consequences in the life of the individual. It also stands for some sort of power or energy generated by an action and having the capacity of bearing consequences. The consequences of the deeds which are stored to be reaped by the performer, start to give result are called Destiny. The power regarded as Fate is nothing but the power of our deeds done in previous existence. The division of Karmas in Indian Philosophy has been lucidly explained by S. C. Chatterjee and D. M. Datta in these words, "According to one principle, karmas are broadly divided into (a) those which have not yet begun to bear fruits (anārabdha karma), and (b) those which have already begun to bear fruits like the present body and its accompaniments (ārabdha or prārabdha karma). Anāradha karma again can be subdivided into two classes, according as it is accumulated from past lives (prāktana or sañcita karma) or is being gathered in this life (Kriyamāna or Sañcīyamāna karma)."[53] So, the accumulated consequences of previous deeds are called Sañcita, and that portion of which has begun to affect and influence our present life and also shapes it is regarded as Prārabdha and this is another name for Destiny or Fate. Thus our past actions influence our present life in the form of Destiny. So, Fate and human effects are not entirely different things but the same Karma, performed earlier in relation to time, but now different in shape.

Whether man is free or not in his performance can be answered by analysing the concept of law of Karma. We have mentioned earlier that the law of Karma asserts the working of the law of causation in the field of morality. It asserts that no one can disown his own deeds if once they are committed. But at the same time it also asserts that every one is free to counteract the effects of those actions by doing other good deeds. So, man is free so long as he has freedom of will to choose different actions and is bound by those effects which are accumulated from his past performances which we call Destiny or Fate. Dr. P. Nagaraja Rao observes in this connection thus, 'Karma is the moral law of causation. It declares that man's will is free, and that he is responsible for all his actions. Nothing that man does is private. Human suffering neither arises of itself nor is unavoidable. What we sow, we reap."[54]

Deeds either performed in the past life or being performed in this life result in pleasure or pain, success or failure. Every one of us faces both favourable and unfavorable situations in life causing both success and failure in result. Every man is himself responsible for such conditions and not his Destiny. It is due to his free choice which he made in his previous life. His choice is determined by his education, character and so on. Even these things are not determined by any supernatural entity but by his previous deeds. The past deeds of the individual influence his choices. Thus, a man himself influences his present and future by receiving the due which is the justified fruit of his action. Maganlal. A. Buch remarks, "The Hindu view, therefore, regards Karma as the central factor, the basic foundation of a man's character and destiny. No blind fate, no mysterious necessity, no high-handed providence predetermined man's actions arbitrarily. But his own past deed, his own Karma, regulates his character, and governs its future developments."[55]

To judge whether man is free or not in his actions, it becomes essential to distinguish between that part which is beyond control in human nature and that which can be controlled and moulded by our motives and intentions. There are certain factors in our life which are guided by forces beyond our control. As for instance, we have no control over the time, place and condition of life where we are born. But we have control over our actions, thoughts, sentiments. In spite of all these limitations we are free to make our choice. We have freedom of will. Dr. Radhakrishnan compares human freedom of will with the freedom of will of the players of the bridge game. He says, "Life is like a game of bridge. We did not invent the game or design the cards. We did not frame the rules and we cannot control the dealing. The cards are dealt out to us whether they be good or bad. To that extent, determinism rules. But we can play the game well or play it badly. A skilful player may have poor hand and yet win the game. A bad player may have a good hand and yet make a mess of it."[56] He further writes, "Our life is a mixture of necessity and freedom, chance and choice. By exercising our choice properly, we can control steadily all the elements and eliminate altogether the determinism of nature."[57] Dr. P. Nagaraja Rao also holds the same view.[58] Pandharinath Prabhu, too recognizes Destiny as the accumulated effect of the past doings.[59] We are free so long as we are at liberty to choose between alternatives and bound so far as our conditions are concerned. However, even these conditions are due to our own choices, which we, had made in previous life.

The epic which believes both in Destiny and human Efforts, attaches more importance to the latter. Human Exertion is primary, because it has the capacity to change or to undo the effects of Destiny. We have mentioned earlier that Destiny is nothing but the stored effects of past deeds. The Hindu ethics believes in the law of Karma which implies freedom of will. It also presupposes the theory of rebirth. Rebirth is possible only when a man is free in his doings and every deed of his must have some effects, as every event must have a cause. If we have performed some deeds, we have sown the seeds and we shall have to reap the due and justified fruits in course of time. If we cannot reap the fruits in the present life; we shall have to take another birth to reap those fruits. This reaping of fruits determines our race, ancestry, parentage, colour, birth-place, social status and other things. Here it seems as if men were not free, because all these are determined by Fate, but actually it is, nothing but the effect of their own previous deeds. It is true that we are not free as regards the circumstances and situations of our present-life, but it is also true that these things have necessarily resulted from our own actions which we did in the previous life. It is not something independent of the individual's own actions. Thus we find a beautiful reconciliation of the apparently conflicting principles of Determinism and Voluntarism.

The Hindu ethics accepts the law of Karma and the theory of rebirth in order to explain Destiny, which is the outcome of the deeds performed freely. However, an individual's efforts alone are not sufficient to affect the course of his life. The roles of heredity and environment are equally significant over which one has no control. For the smooth functioning of society, individuals have to be made responsible, otherwise ethics will become a delusion. The problem is still stirring the minds of those who are engaged in moral pursuits as Libertarians, Hard and Soft Determinists.

Reference

1. Hiriyanna, M., Outlines of Indian Philosophy, p. 118.
2. Ibid., p. 127.
3. Sharma, C.D., A Critical Survey of Indian Philosophy, p. 32.
4. Sabhā, 81, 8-9-10
5. Udyoga, 159, 4-5; P. C. Roy, Ch, 160.
6. Ibid 159, 15.
7. Śānti, 288, 4, Cri, edi, 230. 4.
8. Ibid, 32, 12.
9. Vana, 30, 21-27.
10. Śānti, 235, 10, 8-11; Cri. edi. 219, 10, 8-11.
11. Ibid 224, 14-16; Cri. edi 217, 15, 14-16.
12. Ibid, 224, 25,; Cri. edi. 217, 25.
13. Ibid, 224, 47 51-52,; Cri. edi, 217, 47, 47, 51-52.
14. Śānti, 238, 19-20, Cri. edi, 230, 19-20.
15. Ibid, 33, 22., 33, 16-32.
16. Ibid, 177, 9-10, Cri. edi. 271, 9-10.
17. Udyoga, 39, 1.
18. Ibid, 40, 32.
19. Anu, 163, 1-2.

20. Ibid, 163, 4-5.
21. Āśrama, 10, 27-28.
22. Agrawal, Basudeo Saran, Bhārata Sāvitri, Vol, II, p.6.
23. Ibid., p. 41.
24. Śānti, 279, 12, Cri. edi., 290, 13; P. C. Roy, 294.
25. Udyoga, 29; 6-8.
26. Ibid, 29; 9-16.
27. Śanti, 56, 14-15.
28. Anu, 6, 7 & 10.
29. Ibid, 6, 18, 19, 20 & 28.
30. Ibid, 6, 30-41.
31. Ibid, 6, 47.
32. Vana, 32, 10-15.
33. Śānti, 56, 15 (Bombay Edition).
34. Anu, 6, 43.
35. Anu, 6, 49.
36. Kiṣk, XXV, 1, 4 to 8.
37. Bāla, LVIII, 20 to 23; Kiṣk, XXX, 16-18; Yuddiha, LXXII, 6.
38. Sund, XXXVI, 19.
39. Vana, 32, 46-53.
40. Śānti, 137, 78-80, Cri, edi., 130 82-81.
41. Dey, S.K., The Mahābhārata, Pub. in 'History of philosophy,' Eastern and Western, edi. by. Radhakrishnan, p. 91.
42. Buch, M.A., Principles of Hindu Ethics, p. 549.
43. Vora, D.P., Evolution of Morals in Epics, p. 178.
44. Anu, 1, 21.
45. Ibid, 1, 35-36.
46. Ibid, 1, 37-38.
47. Ibid, 1, 41.
48. Anu, 2, 50-57.
49. Ibid, 1; 70-76.
50. Chandavarkar, G. A., A Manual of Hindu Ethics, p. 62.

51. Valavalkar, Pandharinath, The Hindu Social Philosophy, Pub. in Bhartiya vidya, Vol. II, Part-II, May, 1941.
52. Hopkins, E. W., The Great Epic of India, p. 105.
53. Chatterjee, Satischandra and Datta Dhirendra Mohan, An Introduction to Indian Philosophy, p. 16.
54. Rao, P. Nagaraja., The doctrine of Karma, Pub. in 'The Aryan Path, Vol. 30, 1959, p. 23.
55. Buch, Maganlal A., Principles of Hindu Ethics, p. 572.
56. Radhakrishnan, S., The Bhagavadgītā, p. 49.
57. Ibid., p. 49.
58. Rao, P. Nagaraja., The Doctorion of Karma, Pub. in The Aryan Path, Vol. 30, 1959, p. 26.
59. Prabhu, Pandharinath., Hindu Social Organization, p. 49.

5

The Different Standards of Morality

In the Hindu ethics, we find mentions of several moral standards. They may be discussed under the following heads, which however, are not mutually exclusive but often overlapping and repetitive with differences in points of emphasis according to the nature of the context.

(A) Sukhavāda or Hedonism.

(B) Self--conquest or Rationalism.

(C) Customs and traditions.

(D) Social good

(E) Duty

(F) Vidhi or law.

(G) 'Might is right'.

(H) Behaviour of great men.

(I) Purity of motive.

(J) Mokṣa or self-realisation.

(A) Sukhavāda or Hedonism as a standard of morality:

The standard of Hedonism is recurrently found in the Mahātbhārata. Sukha or pleasure of this world or of the other is primarily regarded as the summum bonum of life. In the dialogue between a bird named Pūjanī and king Brahmadatta, 'sukha' or happiness is accepted as an object of desire. The bird says, "All beings desire pleasure and seek to avoid pain."[1] Saint Bhṛgu also affirms that men always try to avoid pain, and everything is done only for the sake of pleasure. He says to Bharadvāja, "Happiness is said to be of two kinds, viz., bodily and mental. Both in this and the other world, the visible and invisible fruits (of actions) are specified (in the Vedas) for the sake of happiness.... Happiness is desirable.

It is an attribute of the Soul. Both virtue and profit are sought for its sake."[1] In the Anusāśanaparva, Bṛhaspati says to Yudhiṣṭhira, "Endued with 1ife, O king, jiva in this world, from the moment of his birth, enjoys and endures his own (previous) acts, depending upon righteousness (and its reverse). If jīva, according to the best of his power follows righteousness, from the day of his birth, he then succeeds in enjoying, when reborn happiness without interruption."[2] Hence to seek pleasure and avoid pain is repeatedly maintained in the epic. Pleasure and pain both come in the life but one tries to seek pleasure and avoid pain. Thus, the hedonistic ideal of life seems to occupy a prominent position in the epic. Dr. Radhakrishnan also opines, "Ethics as the pursuit of happiness is given an important place in the Mahābhārata."[3]

If we analyse the hedonistic elements in the Mahābhārata, we find different shades of hedonism in it, e.g., psychological and ethical, egoistic and altruistic, gross and refined. The dialogue between the bird Pūjāni and King Brahmadatta shows that seeking of pleasure and avoiding of pain is the natural tendency of living creatures. The discourse between Bhṛgu and Bharadvāja also points out pleasure as the normal object of desire. Such passages in the Mahābhārata clearly advocate psychological hedonism.

In the Śāntiparva when Nārada advises Śuka not to lament for unhappiness and to use all means to obviate pain, he does not regard it as a psychological and normal fact, rather he asks him that he should engage all means to avoid pain. In the Vans parva, it is stated that one should seek pleasure in the first portion of life, wealth in the second, and virtue in the last.[4] Here the word 'should' is used. This is ethical hedonism. When we examine the various shades of hedonistic thought in the Mahābhārata, we find elements of egoism as well as of altruism. In the Anuśāsanaparva, Bhīṣma advises Yudhiṣṭhira to seek his (Yudhiṣṭhira's) own self-interest. Bhīṣma says that those practices that support society, the duties of righteousness and all those acts which are productive of benefit to one's own self, should be performed.[5] Here we find a synthesis of egoism and altruism. In the Vanaparva sage, Mārkaṇḍeya also asks Yudhiṣṭhira to seek his own benefit. He says, "Good men having an eye to their own welfare, as also virtue and the ways of the world, act in this way and thereby grow in virtue through endless ages."[6] The egoistic nature of man is revealed in the fable of the rat and the cat. The rat 'Palita' states to the cat 'Lomaśa': "No body is anybody's foe, nobody is anybody's friends; persons become friend or foes only from motives of interest.... The father, the mother, the son, the maternal uncle, the sister's son, other relatives and kinsmen, are all guided by considerations of interest and profit. The friendship between two uterine brother, the love between husband and wife, depend upon interest. I do not know any kind of affection in any person that does not rest upon some motive of self-interest."[7] This may be compared to a similar trend of thought found in the Bṛhadāraṇyakopaniṣad. Yājñavalkya states to his wife Maitreyī, "O Maitrayī, the husband is loved by the wife, not for the sake of the husband, but for the sake of her own ātman: in the same way, the son is not loved by us for his own sake: we love him for our own sake.... We like all things for the sake of our self (ātman)"[8]

Although there are occasional references to self-interest here and there, the ethical trend of thought in the epic is pronouncedly altruistic. The epic emphasises the other-regarding virtue of 'Do as you would be done by', as the golden rule of life. Vidura enjoins in the Śāntiparva that one should also behave towards all creatures as he should towards himself.[9] This principle is also maintained in the Viduranīti: "That which is antagonistic (adverse) to one's own self should never be applied in respect of another."[10] Bhīṣma observes it, "Knowing how painful it is to himself, a person should never do that to others which he dislikes when done to him by others.... How can one who breathes to live himself think of preventing another from doing the same by a murderous act? Whatever wishes one entertains with respect to one's oneself, one should certainly cherish with respect to another."[11] From the above verses it is obvious that the principle of self-identification with others is the main cause underlying welfare of others. Self-identification is the basis of altruism. So egoism gives way to altruism. To do good or welfare to others is regarded as one of the important aspects of Dharma. In the Vanaparva, Draupadī says that whichever conduces most to the good of all creatures is considered to be truth.[12] At another place in the Śāntiparva, Dhṛtarāṣṭra, after narrating the stories of Prahlāda and Indra, tells his son Duryodhana:- "That act or exertion by which others are not benefited, or that act in consequence of which one has to feel shame, should not be done."[13] Here in place of 'pleasure' we find 'benefit of others' which determines, actions to be done or not. If any act is not beneficial to others, it should not be performed. The intellectual discourse between Tulādhāra and jājali also shows the importance to the welfare of others. Tulādhāra says, "He, O Jājali, is said to know what morality or righteousness is, who is always the friend of all creatures and who is always engaged in the good of all Creatures, in thought, word, and deed."[14] S.N. Gajendragadkar observes in this connection: "It is clear that Tulādhāra is expounding Dharma which has a universal appeal in that. It aims at human welfare, peace in society and personal tranquillity."[15]

In the Gītā also, we find stress on the welfare of all beings. At one place Kṛṣṇa says to Arjuna, "Those Ṛṣis, who have lost the sense of duality (that is, who have realised the principle that there is only one Permeśvara in all places), whose sins have been dissolved, and who have become engrossed in achieving the welfare of the entire creation by means of self-control, attain Release in the shape of Brahma-nirvāṇa."[16] Again at another place he says, "After having controlled their senses and become equable-minded towards everything, such (persons too), who are engrossed in the welfare of all beings, also come and reach Me."[17] Thus we find that the stress is not on the welfare of human beings only but on the welfare of all living creatures. The altruism of the epic is wide enough to cover the whole universe within its scope.

Pleasure is sometimes divided into sensual and intellectual. In the Mahābhārata, we find some passages in support of sensualist hedonism. Bhīma requests his eldest brother Yudhiṣṭhira not to renounce but to enjoy the world. He says, "Approaching beautiful damsels attired in excellent robes, adorned with every ornament, and exhibited with sweet wines, do thou sport with them. Kāma O king, should be the foremost of the three (Artha, Dharma and Kāma) with us."[18] This reminds us of the gross egoistic hedonism of Aristippus. In the epic, we also find some verses advocating preference of present to future pleasure. It is stated that the abandonment of present happiness and the pursuit of that which is yet to come is never the policy of a person possessed of intelligence.[19] It suggests the philosophy of 'eat, drink and be merry for tomorrow you may die.' Thus it can be said that some elements of gross hedonism are traceable in the epic.

We have observed that Bhṛgu makes a distinction between bodily and mental pleasure.[20] A similar distinction is found in the Epicurean ethical philosophy.[21] It is regarded as refined hedonism because it prefers mental pleasure to physical.

Happiness, achieved through reason, is regarded as greater than that achieved through the senses. The Gītā enjoins, "The happines is the most beautific happiness which being obtainable only by means of Reason, is independent of the organ."[22]

We find three kinds of pleasure in the Gītā-Sattva, Rajasa and Tamasa. It enjoins, "That in which one finds enjoyment only through practice (of Bhajana, meditation and worship) whereby one reaches the end of sorrow-nay, that which appears like poison in the beginning (i.e., when the practices are started), but tastes as nectar in the end, born of the placidity of mind brought about by meditation on God, such a joy is said to be Sāttvika. The joy which is derived from the contact of the senses with their objects, though appearing like nectar in the beginning (at the time of enjoyment), proves to be mischievous like poison in the end. That is why such a joy is said to be Rājasika. The joy which deadens the soul, both in the beginning and in the end, and which is derived from sleep, indolence and carelessness is said to be Tāmasika."[23] The first kind of happiness is regarded as the best.

In the epic, there is a distinction between worldly pleasure and heavenly pleasure. Earthly pleasure is mixed with pain where as heavenly pleasure is unalloyed or unmixed. We feel that everybody is constantly struggling with a view to obtaining happiness. He wants pleasure on the one hand and less pain, as much as possible, on the other hand. As a matter of fact, he does not succeed in achieving pleasure without pain and suffering. It is stated in the Mahābhārata that in this world, pain is mixed with happiness.[24] In another context, we find an analogical description that the happiness and sorrow of human beings are revolving like a wheel. Sorrow comes after joy and joy after sorrow.[25] It is stated by Śampāka that diverse kinds of sorrow and happiness overtake, from the day of birth of the person that is born on the earth.[26] Draupadī appears to be correct when she states to Satyabhāmā that happiness never comes out of happiness. In order that a saintly women should experience happiness, she must experience pain and suffering.[27] Pain and suffering are of many kinds. The bird Pūjanī says to king Brhamadatta that misery arises from various sources. Decrepitude is misery. The loss of wealth is misery. The adjacence of anything disagreeable or evil is misery. Separation or dissociation from friends and agreeable objects is misery.[28] In the Śāntiparva, Bhṛgu says that there are both pleasure and pain in this world. They are mixed together. There is unmixed pleasure only in heaven. And the real pleasure is the very nature of the supreme Brahman.[29] Bhṛgu further says that diverse kinds of physical and mental evils are never found in heaven. Pleasure in heaven is permanent and immutable. In heaven delicious breezes blow. There is also perpetual fragrance. There is no hunger, no thirst, no decrepitude, no sin.[30]

Thus according to the epic, the happiness of heaven is pure and superior to worldly pleasure. The former is unalloyed and perennial; the latter is mixed and transient. Nārada says to Śuka that in this unhappiness is greater than happiness.[31] The desire for happiness of the world is not fully satisfied as happiness is supposed to spring from the satisfaction of desires, and all desires cannot be satisfied. Yayāti says that by enjoying objects of pleasure, the desire for the objects of pleasure is not satisfied, but on the other hand, this desire grows more and more, just as fire burns more and more by sacrificial offerings being thrown into it.[32] Hence the epic repeatedly emphasises on Tyāga as a means to obtain happiness according to the measure of the desires one may be able to cast off.[33] Tyāga or sacrifice and contentment are the real ways of getting happiness is also maintained is another context.[34] Nārada says to Śuka, "Nāsi tyāgasamam sukham," i.e., there is no happiness equal to

Tyāga.[35] Thus it appears that even sacrifice is prompted by a desire to get happiness as its reward.

In attaining heaven, there is a desire to enjoy the pleasure available there. J. C. Oman in his book 'The Creat Epic of India,' regards the heaven of Hindu gods as essentially material and sensuous with lively Gandharvas and beautiful Apsara.[36] In this connection Sivaswami Aiyar observes, "The original view was the attainment of happiness in heaven by the performance of religious rites."[37] There is a hedonistic motive behind all rituals. One wants to go to heaven only because he wants to get unmitigated pleasure there. Thus the concept of Svarga (heaven) is essentially hedonistic. Thus the ultimate aim of life seems to be to enjoy pleasure or happiness in this life or hereafter.

(B) Self-conquest or Rationalism as a standard of morality:

Rationalism as a standard of morality is given due importance in the Mahābhārata. According to Rationalism, Reason is the superior element in human nature. It distinguishes men from lower beings. Fulfilment of the higher-self or the rational self is supposed to be the ideal of Rationalism. In the Mahābhārata, we find enough verses supporting Rationalism and directing us to control our lower instinct by reason. In the Śāntiparva, Manu says to Bṛhaspati, "By controlling sense-organs man lives happily and by not controlling them he gets pain. Therefore, sense-organs must be controlled by reason."[38] The control of sense-organ is essential for a man to realise his end. In the Udyogaparva, Vidura advises Dhṛtarāṣṭa to control his sensibility as it leads to different sorts of calamities. He observes: "Like the moon during the lighted fortnight, calamities increase in respect of him who is vanquished by the five senses in their natural state whichever lead him towards various acts."[39]

In the Śāntiparva, Bhīṣma also lays stress on self-restraint which leads to the highest religious merit. He says to Yudhiṣṭhira, "Those amongst the ancients that were acquainted with truth said that self-restraint leads to the highest merit. Through self-restraint a man becomes cleansed of all his sins and endued with energy, and as a consequence, attains to the highest blessedness. We have not heard that there is any other duty in all the worlds that can equal self-restraint. Self-restraint, according to all virtuous persons, is the highest of virtues in this world. Endued with self-restraint, one acquires great virtue. The self-restrained man sleeps in felicity and awakes in felicity, and moves through the world in felicity. His mind is always cheerful."[40] Self-restraint or Dama is thus taken as an essential criterion of morality.

Contrary to the tenets of hedonism or Sukhavāda, premium is put on killing or subduing of desires and feelings. Animal-self is advised to be conquered by subjugating desires. In the epic, we find repeated requests to give up desires as they are the sources of all miseries. In the Śāntiparva, Brāhmiṇ advises to Senajit, "Whatever objects amongst things that are desired, are cast off become sources of happiness. The man that pursues objects of desires meets with destruction in course of the pursuit... When a person succeeds in withdrawing all its limbs, then his should, which is self-luminous succeeds in looking into itself."[41] Again in the Maṇkigītā, Maṇki attaches more importance to giving up of desires than to get satisfaction of desires. He says, "Amongst these two, viz., one who obtains the fruition of all his wishes, and who casts off every wish, the latter, who renounces all, is superior to the former who obtains the fruition of all."[42]

In the Gītā, Kṛṣṇa describing the state of Sthitaprajña advises Arjuna to control his senses to have stability of mind. He thus says, "When like a tortoise, which draws in its limbs from all directions, he withdraws his senses from the sense-objects, his mind has become stable... Turbulent by nature, the senses even of a wise man, who is practising self-control, forcibly carry away his mind, Arjuna. Therefore having controlled them all and collecting his mind, one should sit for meditation devoting oneself heart and soul to Me. For he whose senses are mastered, his mind has become stable."[43] Kṛṣṇa points out to Arjuna how desires ruin a man. In this connection Kṛṇṣa says, "The man dwelling on sense-objects develops attachment for them; from attachment springs up desire,and from desire (unfulfilled) ensues anger. From anger arises infatuation; from infatuation, confusion of memory; from confusion of memory, loss of reason; and from loss of reason one goes to complete ruin."[44] At the end of the chapter Kṛṣṇa states, "He, who gives up all desires and moves free from attachment, egoism and thirst for enjoyment, attains peace."[45]

For controlling the sense-organs, the epic advises up to rely upon Reason or Buddhi. Bhīṣma says to Yudhiṣṭhira that wisdom is the refuge of creatures. Wisdom is regarded as the highest of acquisitions. Wisdom is the highest felicity in the world. Wisdom is heaven in the estimation of good and virtuous. It is through wisdom that Bali, Prahlāda, Namuci and Maṅki, when they lost their (earthly) prosperity, succeed in acquiring felicity. What is there that is superior to wisdom?[46] At another place, he takes everything as a manifestation of Intelligence."[47] In the Śāntiparva, Manu says that as when quantity of water is clear, images reflected in it can be seen by the eyes, after the same manner, if the senses be unperturbed, the soul is capable of being viewed by the understanding. If, however, the quantity of water gets stirred, the person standing by it can no longer see those images. Similarly, if the senses become perturbed, the soul can no longer be seen by the Understanding. Ignorance begets delusion. Delusion affects the Mind. When the Mind becomes vitiated, the five senses which have the Mind for their refuge become vitiated also. Surcharged with ignorance, and sunk in the mire of worldly objects, one cannot enjoy the sweets of contentment or tranquillity".[48] In the Kāmagītā, Kṛṣṇa says to Yudhiṣṭhira that men do not took with approbation upon the conduct of those who are engrossed in worldly desires and there is no act without having a desire (as its root) and all (Kāma) desires are, as it were, the limbs (off shoots) of the mind. Therefore, wise men knowing this subjugate their desires.[49]

A similar tendency is noticed in Buddhism. To give up desire and release from pain is regarded as the supreme virtue. According to Buddha the root of all actions is desire. Hence, desires should be destroyed and only then there will be the end of all sufferings and sorrows. Prof. M. Hiriyanna explains the Buddhistic conception of self-abnegation thus, "The very desire for them (Buddhists) is a delusion and we should, therefore, wean ourselves from it as quickly as possible. More powerful than this desire for outside things is the craving for the preservation of the self or the will to be. Buddhism teaches that since there is no self at all, we should first get rid of this craving, if we have to extinguish the pains of existence. Thus self-denial is to be understood in a literal sense in Buddhistic ethics... With the negation of self, all selfish impulses necessarily disappear."[50] In the epic, the control of sense-organs is emphasised to avoid pain and suffering of the universe. It is observed that it is the reason which can control sense-organs and make life a rational life a moral life. Morality consists in this subordination of lower instinct to reason.

Reason (Buddhi) and Mind (Manasa) are taken as the means to control the sense-organs. It is stated by Manu in the epic that knowledge comes out of Brahman, reason from knowledge, and Mind from Reason and then Mind experiences objects with sense-organs.[51] It is also stated by Vyāsa that the objects of senses or qualities are superior to the sense-organs (because they forcibly attract them towards themselves). The

Mind (Manasa) is superior to those objects (as it succeeds in detracting these sense-organs from those objects). The Understanding is superior to Mind. The Soul is regarded as superior to Understanding.[52] About Reason it is stated by Vyāsa in the Śāntiparva, "The Understanding takes different shapes or form to get objects within it. When the Understanding, of its own motion, forms ideas (of objects) within itself, it then comes to be called Mind... When it hears, it becomes the organ of hearing, and when it touches, it becomes the organ of touch. Similarly, when it sees, it becomes the organ of vision and when it tastes, it becomes the organ of taste, and when it smells it becomes the organ of scent. It is the Understanding that appears under different guises (for different functions) by modification."[53] Vyāsa holds that there are three prompting forces behind voluntary action. First, Mind creates several feelings, then Reason decides it, then heart feels its necessity and then an action is performed.[54] Thus we find that Mind and Reason are important factors in determining actions of the life.

The relation between mind and reason is nicely described by B. G. Tilak. He says, "The Reason in its capacity of a judge, necessarily becomes superior to the Mind and the Mind becomes the clerk of the Reason. This is the purport of the following words used in the Gītā, namely. 'Manasastu para buddhih". 'the Reason is superior to or beyond the Mind (Gītā 3-42). Nevertheless, even this clerk has, as mentioned above, to perform two different functions; the first of these is to properly arrange all the impressions which have come from outside, through the medium of the organs of perception: and to place those impressions before the Reason for decision: and the second one is to carry the order or the message of the Reason to the organs of Action after the Reason has arrived at a decision, and makes those organs perform those external actions which are necessary to be performed for carrying out the decision of the Reason,"[55] Such distinction is also noticed in the epic. In the

Śāntiparva, Vyāsa states that the Understanding or Buddhi is an organ which does the 'vyavsāyaḥ' i. e., which discriminates and arrives at a decision and the Mind (Manasa) is an organ which does the 'Vyākaraṇam' i, e., carries out the development or the further arrangements.[56]

No doubt, there is difference between Mind and Reason, but both of them are essential for controlling the sense-organs. It is true that Reason does control it but it has also to take the help of the mind for having control over those sense-organs. It is Understanding which helps man in attaining salvation. Vyāsa says to Śuka, "The senses that are maddening should carefully be restrained by the Understanding like a sire restraining his own inexperienced children liable to fall into diverse evil habits. The withdrawal of the Mind the senses from all unworthy objects and their due concentration (upon worthy objects) is the highest penance. That is the foremost of all duties. Indeed, that is said to be the highest duty."[57] He further states, "Directing, by the aid of the Understanding, the senses having the Mind for their sixth, and without, indeed, thinking of worldly objects which have the virtue of inspiring innumerable kind of thought, one should live contented with one's own self. When the senses and the Mind, withdrawn from the pastures among which they usually run loose, come back for residing in their proper abode, it is then that thou wilt behold in thy own self the Eternal and Supreme Soul."[58] Thus we find that Reason has been given a very high place in the ethics propounded in the epic.

(C) Customs and Traditions as a standard of morality:

In the Mahābhārata on several occasions, we find that right and wrong actions are judged by the prevailing customs and traditions of the community. Naturally, they are regarded as a standard of morality in the epic, S. K. Maitra defines tradition as a standard of morality in this way, "Lokopadeśa,

Tradition, is the standard according to those who hold that morality consists in the longstanding customs and usages that obtain amongst people."[59] In the fifth chapter of the Ādiparva when the question is raised whether Pulomā's husband is saint Bhṛgu or the giant named Pulomā, Agni gives his verdict in favour of the saint. Agni regards their marriage as legal and justified because it has taken place traditionally and according to the custom by uttering Mantras. Agni states, "This Pulomā was, indeed first chosen by thee, O Rākṣasa, but she was not taken by thee with holy rites and invocations.

But this far-famed lady was bestowed by her father on Bhṛgu as a gift from desire of blessing. She was not bestowed on thee. O Rākṣasa this lady was duly made by the sage Bhṛgu his wife with Vedic rites in my presence. This is she- I know her."[60] In the same Parva, we notice that the forefathers of Jaratakāru are lying in hell only because he is not celebrating his marriage ceremony which is the convention and he is thus destroying the tradition.[61]

Sometimes it becomes difficult to choose the right path of morality when two of them disagree. In such situations, we have to take the help of tradition and custom to avoid wrong path. In the epic on many occasions, we cannot pass moral judgement over actions without taking the help of this standard. As for instance, it becomes troublesome to decide whether all the five Pāṇḍavas are justified in marrying Draupadī simultaneously following the wishes of their mother Kunti. King Drupada, father of Draupadī and her brother Dhṛṣṭadyumna are against such marriage. Drupada states, "In my opinion this marriage is in contravention of morality because it is antagonistic to the Vedas and customs.. There is no custom like this that so many persons should keep one wife."[62] Thus Drupada takes it as immoral action. But Yudhiṣṭhira justifies their polyandry. Both take their stand on time-honoured customs and traditions. Yudhiṣṭhira says, "The course of nature of Dharma is very subtle, so we do not know the dharma's course, but we must follow our forefathers."[63] He quotes a precedent from the Puraṇas that a most pious girl named Jatilā was married to seven saints at a time.[64] He cites another example of Vārkṣī the daughter of saint Kaṇdu who was married to ten Persons, all brothers and having the same name.[65] On the basis of these evidences, he says that the marriage of Draupadī with Pāṇḍavas is sanctioned by tradition and therefore unimpeachable.

The life of people in the epic period was supposed to be governed by the traditions and customs prevailing in society. These traditions and customs were in keeping with the status and condition of the persons concerned. A king had to follow the tradition of his royal family, otherwise his actions would be condemned. Similarly, a Brāhmiṇ had to observe the customs and traditions of his class. In the Sāntiparva, we find that some Brāhmiṇ boys of rich families leave their home and start to lead a saintly life in the forest. One day Indra comes in the from of a golden bird and asks them to go back home. He states that there is a provision of duties pertaining to the class and sacraments or Saṁskāras with Mantras for the Brāhmiṇs. As long as they live, they should perform their sacrments. Even after their death the sacraments or ritual ceremonies of burning the dead bodies and other sacraments like Śrāddha should be performed in accordance with the Vedic customs.[66]

In the Śāntiparva, Bhīmasena advises Yudhiṣṭhira to follow the custom and tradition of their forefathers when Yudhiṣṭhira after battle wants to renounce the world and decides not the rule the kingdom. Bhīmasena says, "Applying the intellect to this, and ascertaining that right and the wrong paths of creatures, follow thou the course adopted by thy sire before thee and govern properly thy kingdom."[67] On the same occasion Arjuna requests his eldest brother to rule the kingdom observing the course of the world.[68]

When we go through the different Parvas (Cantos) of the epic dealing with military operations, we find that from its beginning to end, the majority of the performances were observed in accordance with the customs of warfare. In the Śāntiparva, Bhīṣma asks Yudhiṣṭhira to follow the path of his grand-father and great grandfather. He observes, "Follow the conduct of thy sire and grand-sire. Kings should never adopt that conduct which thou desirest to adopt.'[69]

It may be mentioned in this context that the customs and traditions of the Mahābhārata are derived mostly from the Vedas and Smṛtis. They are usually in the form of rigid conventions. Sometimes they also conflict with each other. Customs and traditions are the determinants of actions when other criteria fail.

(D) Social Good as a standard of morality:

Another important standard of morality in the epic is the achievement of social good. The ideal of social good occupies a prominent position in the Mahābhārata. This ideal can be attained only when social equilibrium is maintained, i.e., the four classes of society and the four stages of life should be maintained properly. Social stability is essential for the physical, moral and spiritual growth of the individual. It is stated in the Śāntiparva that for the growth and advancement of the creatures Dharma is essential, "Prabhavārthāya bhūtanāṁ dharmapravacanaṁ kṛtam."[70] It is also stated by Utathya in the epic that Brahmā created Dharma for the welfare of all creatures.[71]

Very often social good is regarded as an essential factor in the determination of right and wrong. Naturally other standards like customs and traditions, law and duty, etc., become secondary as they may be easily included in the prime test of social good. In the Vanaparva, it is stated by the virtuous fowler that untruth sometimes leads to the truth, and the latter dwindles into untruth. Whichever conduces most to the good of all creatures is considered to be truth.[72] Nārada states to Gālaba that he regards welfare of the creatures as truth.[73] It appears from the above illustrations that the criterion of truth is the welfare of creatures.

Morality is supposed to be related with the welfare of society. The individual and society are mutually interdependent. We have discussed that Dharma leads to prosperity and salvation of the individual. The prosperity of the individual is useless and meaningless without society. Individual's prosperity has significance only when society progresses and prospers. Society is supposed to be an organism and its individuals are different limbs. Can working of the organs be active when the organism itself becomes inactive? The answer is in the negative. Similarly, without the good of society, without maintaining welfare of society, no good or welfare of the particular individual can be maintained. Hence, social equilibrium and social stability are supposed to be essential for the betterment of the individual when he takes his birth, receives his education and discharges all sorts of duties in life. Keeping it in view, Bhīṣma states in the Śantiparva that great sages and seers have established Dharma for Lokoyātrā or the maintenance of society.[74] Again it is observed in the same parva by Utathya, 'dharme tiṣṭhati bhūtāni', i.e. even all beings are supported in their existence by Dharma.[75]

Moralty is the guiding principle of society. If it is withdrawn, society as such will cease to exist and there will be anarchy. Bal Gangadhara Tilak observes, "When this Dharma ceases to be observed, the binding ropes of society may be said to have become loose and when these binding ropes are loosened, society will be in the same position as the planetary system consisting of the Sun and the planets would in the sky without the binding force of gravitation or as a ship would be on the ocean without a rudder."[76] In this connection, S. K. Patcliffe states, "Dharma includes the whole social conception of law and conduct and worship. Dharma is the force or principle that binds together; the union of traditional thought and faith of common custom, loyalty and understanding, that makes of society as an arganic or religious whole.'[77] So, Dharma is the cementing force for social unity it is essential for the good functioning of society as a whole.

Dr. Surama Dasgupta, while summarizing the different standards of morality in the Mahābharata" recognizes social good as one of them. To Dasgupta, there are three types of standards of morality in the epic. She takes the advancement of society, maintenance of social-order, preservation of traditions and customs as the first type while final liberation as the second and rules of guidance for the people in abnormal times as the third. Dasgupta states, "The first type is concerned with the well-being of society and the individual, with which the third is also in full consonance, as it aims at the preservation of life and its well-being in times of danger, disorder and anarchy; while the second type is qute different from them; it has as its aim, the freedom of the individual from the bondage of the world (saṁsāra) and, therefore, of society, so to speak. While the first and third ones aim at social welfare and its stability, the second is confined to individual liberation, which is something beyond society, and therefore, may be taken as supra-social.[78]

From the above account, it is clear that Dr. Dasgupta takes the ethics of the epic to be pre-eminently social in character. To her, morality is necessary for social well-being. She states, 'Dharma has been defined as that which supports and sustains the wold."[79] Further she states, "The definition is so elastic that whatever is conducive to the good of the people can be regarded as right and virtue."[80] Thus the concept of Dharma is a social phenomenon having its sway over social working and social betterment.

Much significance is attached to the Varṇāśramadharmas in the epic. They are emphasised only because if the Brāhmiṇ, Kṣatriya, Vaiśya and the Śūdra do not perform their duties, the maintenance of society, stability of social order will disappear and there will be all chaos and confusion. Barbarism and anarchy will prevail in society. Thus it appears that the main aim of the ancient Hindu literatures like the Vedas, Smṛtis, Dharmaāśstras and of the epic is to propound such notion of Dharma which can maintain peace, plenty, and progress of all individuals along with the social stability. The underlying idea is to achieve social good and progress in a harmonious manner. Each class while fulfilling its separate functions fulfils automatically the functions of society. Taken together, these classes work for general welfare as they are related among themselves for the purpose of social unity. Pandhari Nath Valavalkar also has the same opinion when he holds, "The varṇa scheme could be said to promote social organisation in another direction also. It seeks to promote social equilibrium and solidarity through the economic organisation... On the whole, therefore, the varṇa-theory was devised with a view to engage the different types of human energies in different channels suitable to each of them and all towards the one end of social organisation and social stability."[81]

The implication of political morality is the maintenance of peace, justice, progress, law and order in society. Political institutions like Kingship is required to establish social equilibrium and stability to help individuals in performing moral acts. It also helps man in achieving his goals through social orders. For this reason it is stated in the epic that the foremost duty of the king is to preserve and conserve the duties of the four classes.[82]

Aurobindo observes that the earnest desire of the author of the epic is to concentrate upon the social problems like social stability and others. He says, "But Vyāsa has not only a high political and religious thought and deep-seeing social judgement, he deals not only with the massive aspects and worldwide issues of human conduct, but has a keen eye for the details of government and society, the ceremonies, form and usages, the religious and social order and the due stability of which public welfare is governed."[83]

Now judging all these points, it is obvious that the social good is given a great importance in the epic as a standard of morality.

(E) Duty as a standard of morality:

Duty as a standard of morality occupies a prominent position in the Hindu ethics. An action is right if it is in accordance with duty. So, right or wrong, moral or immoral, good or bad actions are judged by the sense of duty and how they are discharged. If an act is done for the sake of duty it is right; if not, it is wrong.

In the epic as we have already seen, duties follow from the birth and rank of the individual. They are determined by the situation and state of the man. If a King, who discharges the duties of a renouncer, while he is a king, he is not true to his own duty. He must follow Rājadharmas which are the proper duties assigned to him.

After war when Yudhiṣṭhira decides not to rule the kingdom but to renounce the world as a renouncer, he is told by all his relatives and preceptors that this determination of his is wrong as it does not agree with the royal duty. Arjuna requests him to rule the kingdom and to perform his duties as a king. He says, "O son of Kuntī, please perform sacrifices, offer gifts, protect your subjects, follow dharma continuously, kill the enemies and have friendship with friends."[84] So, Yudhiṣṭhira seems to be wrong as he is not performing his duties. His actions are wrong as they are not in accordance with his royal status.

In the Mahābhārata, as we have observed earlier, duties of individuals are prescribed according to their classes in society and stages in life. An action is right if it is performed by the individual from a sense of duty. What we want to maintain here is that to follow duties for duty's sake is a standard of morality to judge actions as right or wrong. The Bhagavadgītā teaches us to perform our duties which outweigh all other considerations. In the eighteenth chapter, Kṛṣṇa declares that every man by offering himself completely to the task of performing duty attains perfection.[85] Again at another place he states, "By worshiping him through the performance of his own duty, man attains Perfection."[86] There are many more verses in the Gītā which emphasise the performance of duties assigned according to the class and stage of the individual. In the second chapter Kṛṣṇa advises Arjuna to fight as it is his duty. He observes, "Considering your own duty you should not waver; for there is nothing more welcome for a man of warrior class than a righteous war."[87] Again in the eighteenth chapter he holds, "Better one's own duty, though devoid of merit, than the duty of another well-executed. He who performs 'the duty enjoined by his own nature, does not incur sin."[88]

The epic contains injunctions to the effect that the sense of duty must be preferred to worldly good and even life itself. It is observed by Vidura in the Udyogaparva, "O son, I would impart thee another sacred lesson which is the highest of all teachings, i.e., duty which would never be forsaken for desire, fear or temptation, not for the sake of life itself."[89]

The Gītā enjoins, "Perform always your duties without-regard for the fruits. He who does his duty without attachment attains the Supreme."[90] According to the Gītā that sacrifice is regarded as Sāttvika (proceeding from pure motive), which is performed without any desire or reward and solely from a sense of duty because it is prescribed by the scripture.[91] In the Vanaparva also we find Yudhiṣṭhira exhorting the performance of duty for its own sake. He points out that he does not perform any action with an eye to reward; but because. It is his duty to do it.[92] Thus, the epic upholds the sense of duty as an important standard of morality.

(F) Law as a standard of morality:

'Vidhi' or 'Law' is also taken as a standard of morality in the Hindu ethics. An action is right if it agrees with the law and it is wrong when it violates the law. From the earliest period of our life we find ourselves amidst rules or laws which are prescribed by parents, teachers, guardians, sages and rulers. The term 'Law' includes political law, social law, religious law and moral law in itself. Almost all human conducts appear to be regulated and governed by these laws. Our behaviour to be right and moral, must be in conformity with these laws. In the Mahābhārata we come across such laws as commands of kings, steers and saints, divines, and of the Vedas.

'Vidhi' as the Command of the king: The rule of law imposed by the king, who is the highest earthly authority is taken as the standard of political morality. The royal injunctions constitute duties just as the king's prohibition constitutes the opposite. The king by his 'Daṇḍanīti' or Law of Punishment or chastisement keeps everything on right track.[93] It is stated by Arjuna that "Daṇḍe sthitāh Prajāḥ", i.e., "the people are maintained and sustained by this Daṇḍa.[94] In the same parva, he observes that a sinner does not commit sin for fear of being punished.[95] He further States that chastisement is ordained by the creator himself for protesting religion and profit for the happiness of all four orders, and for making them righteous and modest.[96] It is also stated by him that law governs people and also safeguards their interests.[97]

This reminds us of the Cārvāka view that the earthly king is the only king, there is no lord or God other than him.[98]

The will of the sovereign determines right and wrong as the king is the highest authority. The Mahābhārata, however, is pronouncedly theistic and takes the king as a representative of God.

Commands of seers and saints: In the epic, the injunctions of the great men, seers, and saints are very often takan as guiding principles to decide the moral conflicts and determine the path of performing righteousness. Seers like Vyāsa, Bṛhāspatī, Vīdura, Bhīṣma, king Janaka are taken as authorities and their injunctions are regarded as standards of moral judgement.

According to the Buddhists and Jainas also, it is not the prescriptions of the king, but the injunctions and prohibitions of Buddhas and Arhats that constitute right and wrong. The authority of moral law is spiritual and not Physical, and can be vested only in the seer, i.e., the spiritual expert that has attained perfection by self-culture.[99]

Vidhi as Divine Command: In the epic, we not only get materials in support of royal command and the Commands of saints and seers, but also instances in support of divine law. Like Nyāya-Vaikśiṣkas, Ramanujists and other theists, the Mahābhārata also admits the law of righteousness prescribed by God who is the Creator and moral Governor of the world. Right and wrong, good and bad are determined by the injunctions and prohibitions of scriptures. Vidhi as divine command embodied in scriptural prescriptions constitutes the moral code. It is observed by Bhīṣma in the Śāntiparva that when Dharma decayed and the people gave up studies of the Vedas, and all Vedic knowledge disappeared and all ritual sacrifices vanished, then Brahmā himself composed a moral code named NItiśāstra in which he dealt with all the ends and means-Dharma, Artha, Kāma and Mokṣa. It was composed in one lakh chapters. After that Śaṁkara condensed the Nitiśatra in ten thousand chapters and was called 'Vaiṣālakṣa'. Then again it was condensed by Indra in five thousand chapters which was called 'Bahudantaka'. Again Bṛhaspati abridged it in three thousand chapters which was called Nitiśāstra of Bṛhaspati. Again it was shortened by Śukhrācārya in one thousand chapters. Thus for the benefit and longer life of people, the great saints summarised this Śāstra.[100] So Nitiśāstra is the outcome of the labour of both deities and great saints and seers. Hence it has been given a divine status.

'Vidhi as command of the Vedas': The commands or injunctions of the Vedas constitute of moral code. According to the Mahābhārata, people were living peacefully according to their Dharma. They had been following their Dharma without any external pressure.[102] But a question arises from where does Dharma come? In reply to this question, the epic asserts that the Vedas are the sources of law. Second to the Vedas. Smṛtis are the sources of law. And when the Smṛtis are silent, the path led by the great men is its sources.[103] It is also observed by Bhīṣma in the Śāntiparva that Dharma prevailing in society will be destroyed when the Vedas and rules of punishment are destroyed.[104] So all these laws governing human actions in society are derived from the Vedas.

Though the Mahābhārata is itself sometimes regarded as the source of law, it is not the primary source in itself. It is the impersonal Vedas which are the ultimate source of these Vidhis.[105]

Thus Vidhi as command of the Vedas is regarded impersonal prescription. The communicator of the Vedas only declares the law and does not create it by his will. Vidhi as command of king or saints and seers is of the nature of personal prescription. To S. K. Maitra, the standard is also conceived by the Hindus as a law or command which again is regarded either as a personal prescription of a superior to an inferior being (Paurṣeya) or again as impersonal law (apaurṣeya) without a law giver.[105] Thus, Vidhi as personal or impersonal prescription is an important standard of morality in the epic.

(G) 'Might is right' as a standard of morality:

The next standard in the epic is 'might is right'. When we say 'might is right' it means whatever a stronger man does it is right. In the primal state of Nature issues were decided by physical strength. It is said, "They will take who have the power and those will keep who can". There was no moral sanction of any kind. People devoured one another and no one had a sense of security of life and property. The stronger would swallow the weaker as stronger fishes eat the weaker ones and a bigger one devours the smaller one in the high water. This is called Matsya-Nyāya. Arjuna finds this state of nature in every society. He observes. "I do not behold any creature in the world that supports life without doing any act of injury to others. Animals live upon animals, the stronger upon the weaker"[106]. It is a state where there is no concept of justice. Right and wrong do not exist at all. This is a state of moral anarchy.

In the Mahābhārata, we get some verses which attach more importance to might than to Dharmas. Bhīṣma also supports the value of might. Reason, justice, and duty appear to be worthless before it. To him, physical force is above all, Bhīṣma puts his arguments thus, "No body in this world ever sees the fruits of righteousness and unrighteousness. A Kṣatriya, therefore should seek the acquisition of power. He that is powerful is the master of everything."[107] He regards power as superior to Dharma. He says, "If, however, the two be compared, power will appear to be superior to righteousness. It is from power that righteousness springs. Righteousness rests upon power as all immobile things upon the earth. As smoke depends upon the wind (for its motion), even so righteousness depends upon power. Righteousness which is the weaker of the two as a climbing plant depends for its support upon a tree."[108] Dharma is very subtle and one cannot obtain at once the result of that Dharma performed by the individual. On the contrary, might gives its fruits just after it is applied in work. It is said. "Those persons have enjoyment under their control who have such objects giving enjoyment. Similarly even Dharma is under the control of those who are mightier or stronger. There is nothing impossible for the mighty men, everything of them is pure."[109] It is significant to note the observation made by Bhīṣma about 'might is right'. In the Sabhāparva, Draupadī puts the questions to the Kauravas as to why she was dragged by Duḥśāsana in the court being the wedded wife of the Pāṇḍavas, hailing from the equal status of dynasty to which they belonged. She wants to know whether she has been really won by Duryodhana and has become his maid-servant. In answer to these questions, the learned Bhīṣma states, "What in this world a strong man calls morality is regarded as such by others, however otherwise it may really be; but what a weak man calls morality is scarcely regarded as such even if it be the highest morality."[110]

Might is regarded as essential for statecraft. Might is useful to gain some easily obtainable material things. It is necessary for acquiring kingdom. When any one is stronger than his enemies, only then he can enjoy the happiness and pleasure after getting that kingdom. If he is weak, he will surely be overpowered by other kings and by his foes who have attraction for his riches and kingdom. Without power, a king cannot safeguard his subjects from robbers, anti-social and anti-national elements. He cannot even protect the treasury of his kingdom, without might. A powerless king is no king at all. No one in his kingdom will regard him as his king. If a king is unable to carry on his royal duties, he has no right to be called a king at all. In the words of Bhīṣma, "How can a weak king have a treasury? How again can a king who has no treasury have a strength? How can a weak man have a kingdom? Whence again can one without a kingdom obtain prosperity?"[111] To discharge royal duties, it is essential to possess strength. Power or might is a means for establishing peace and progress in society. In the Udyogaparva, Vidura enlists five types of strength. He speaks to Dhṛtarāṣṭra, 'Men are said to have five different kinds of strength. Of these, the strength of arms is regarded to be of the most inferior kind. Blessed be thou, the acquisition of good counsellors is regarded as the second kind of strength. The wise men have said that the acquisition of wealth is the third kind of strength, The strength of birth, O king, which one naturally acquireth form one's sire and grand-sires, is regarded as the fourth kind of strength. That, however, O Bhārata, by which all these are won and which is the foremost of all kinds of strength, is called the strength of the intellect."[112] Here physical force is regarded as inferior.

Might in the state of Nature and might employed in civilised society for administrative purpose, are different as they are actuated by different motives. In the former case, might is applied for self-aggrandisement and man becomes animal by using blind force in achieving his selfish objective. He does not take the trouble of utilising reason to choose the right path. In the latter case, when a man functions as a social, rational and moral being, force or might is employed by political institutions to establish rule of law and serve the ends of justice. It helps man restore law and order in society. There is application of force in both the cases. In this regard Arjuna says, "If chastisement were abolished from the world, creatures would soon be destroyed. Like fishes in the water, stronger animals prey on the weaker."[113] Thus the state of nature or the state of might is pre-ethical stage of human evolution.

In the epic, we find that might or force is not left free to pay its disastrous role in society but is allowed only within specific limits with a broad goal of individual and social benefits. As

Bhīṣma says, "If righteousness and power be associated with truth, they can then rescue men from great peril."[114]

(H) Behaviour of great men as a standard of morality:

Another important standard of morality which is marked in the epic is 'Behaviour of Great men'. There are occasions in life when we have to perform our acts in the light of the behaviour of the great, learned and high-ranked men of society. We take their actions as precedents and follow them. We regard those precepts as standards because such great and learned men are expected to know what is wrong and what is right. They possess superior knowledge and better insight in judging rightness and wrongness of actions. This standard is recommended by Yudhiṣṭhira in the Vanaparva. At the end of the Parva, there is a story. When Sahadeva, Nakula and Bhīma who had gone to fetch drinking water did not return in time, Yudhiṭṣhira himself went there. He was asked some questions by Yakṣa with a condition that he would be allowed to take water only when he answered his questions. One of the questions was what is the path[115] (of morality)? Yudhiṣṭhira's reply reveals that the path followed by the great men is the path. He says, 'Arguments lead to no certain conclusion, the Srutis are different form one another; there is not even one sage whose opinion can be accepted by all; the truth about religion and duty is hidden in caves; therefore, that alone is the path along which the great have trod.[116] Yudhiṣṭhira regards this standard as commendable and competent to judge human actions. In the Salyaparva, Kṛṣṇa also recommends it as a standard of morality. While justifying the death of the great warriors like Bhīṣma, Droṇa, Karṇa and Bhūriśravā and others by deceitful means he says, "When the number of one's foes is great, then, destruction should be effected by contrivances and deceitful means. The gods themselves, in slaying Asuras, have trod the same way. That way therefore, that hath been trod by the gods, may be trod by all."[117]

King Śivi is famous for his munificence. Once a pigeon followed by a hawk comes to seek the shelter of the king for the safety of its own life. Seeing the hawk which is not ready to spare the life of pigeon, he starts giving his own flesh equivalent to the weight of the pigeon.[118] Thus he sets an example of charity and self-sacrifice. At one place, he explains his benevolent act in this manner, "It was not for fame, nor for wealth, nor from desire of acquiring objects of enjoyment that I did all this. This course is not sinful. It is for this that I do all this. The path which is trodden by the virtuous is laudable. My heart always inclineth towards such a course."[119] He treats offering, gifts as a way of life because that is the path which has been followed previously by good persons.

Thus it is clear from the above facts that Yudhiṣṭhira and King Śivi accept the paths followed by great and venerable men. When the question of rightness and wrongness arises, and it becomes difficult to determine the ethical behaviour, we take into the consideration, the path followed by great men.

Again in the Gītā, we are advised to follow the path shown by great men. In the third chapter, Kṛṣṇa himself observes, "For whatever a great man does, that very thing other men also do, whatever standard he sets the generality of men follow the same."[120] Kṛṣṇa also asks Arjuna to follow standards preached or adopted by great men and also those standards which he himself propounds as a divine being. He very clearly states that he (Kṛṣṇa) himself adopts those things which do not harm the world because men follow him (Kṛṣṇa) in all fields of life. He says, "should I not engage in action, unwearied at all times, great harm will come to the world, for, Arjuna, men follow my path in all matters."[121] Commenting on these two instances, H. N. Mishra remarks, "These two instances show us that the Gītā believes in the authority of learned persons in matters of moral dispute. Moreover, this principle of practical guidance is not an invention of the Bhagavadgītā but it is found in almost all the sacred texts of the Hindus."[122]

In the Mahābhārata, it is repeatedly mentioned that Dharma follows from the Vedas, Smṛtis, and behaviour laid down by great reverend men. It is also stated by Vyāsa that to get pleasure of both the worlds - worldly and other worldly, men must follow the path paved by great men.[123] It has been emphasised in the epic at several places. There are many stories which strengthen the point that path paved by great men is the standard of morality. The intellectual discourse between Tulādhāra and Jājali lays stress on the behaviour of great and good men as an ethical standard. Tulādhāra citing his own case says to Jājali, "I follow the practices of high-soul and benevolent men of advanced years who with their children and children's children live in the due observance of the ordinance laid down in the scriptures.... That wise man who, having restrained his senses, practiseth, with a heart cleansed from all desires of injuring others, the conduct that is followed by those called good, is sure, O Jājali, to acquire the merit of righteousness (and emancipation which is its fruits)."[124] Tulādhāra pointing out the subtle nature of Dharma states further, "The subject of duties hath many secrets and mysteries. It is so subtle that it is not easy to understand it fully. Amongst diverse conflicting ordinances, some succeed in comprehending duty observing the acts of the good."[125] In the Rāmāyaṇa also, we find that Rāma advocates it as a standard of morality. When Lakṣamaṇa becomes angry and asks Rāma to get the throne by force. Rāma pacifies him by saying that Dharmic path which was trod by great forefathers be trod by them.[126]

Thus precepts and practices of the great men become precedents and serve as beckon-light which guides our conduct. Thus the path of the great is accepted in the epic as a respectable standard of morality.

(I) Purity of motive as a standard of morality:

Purity of motive is also treated as a standard of morality in the Hindu ethics. According to this standard, an action should not be judged by its result, but by the motive behind the action. Unlike hedonism which attaches significance to the consequences of the action, it gives importance to the intention of the doer. We find that the Mahābhārata suggests not only those standards of morality according to which moral judgements are based upon consequences but it also offers such standards which determine actions to be right or wrong on the basis of motives. It indicates that rightness does not depends merely upon the happiness and goodness of others and of the self. Similarly, wrongness does not depends merely on the unhappiness of others and of the self. Rightness and wrongness proceed from the purity and impurity of motives which determine actions. S. K. Maitra puts it thus, "Hence happiness and unhappiness, whether of self or of others, cannot of themselves constitute righteousness and unrighteousness. It is only when such happiness or unhappiness arises from the purity and impurity of the motives prompting the actions which cause them that there is righteousness or unrighteousness."[127]

In the Āśvamedikaparva, there is a story which brings out purity of motive as a standard of morality. When Yudhiṣṭhira performs the Aṣvamedha Yajña (ritul sacrifice) and millions of people are satisfied and begin to praise the magnificent food and gifts, a blue eyed mongoose (Nakula), with one side of his body changed into gold, comes there and speaks in a thunderous voice, "Ye king, this seat sacrifice is not equal to a prastha of powdered barley given away by a liberal Brāhmiṇ of Kurukṣetra who is observing the Unccha vow."[128] The story is that a Brāhmiṇ along with his wife, son and daughter-in-law offered their shares of powdered barley to a hungry guest (a mendicant) who came when they were to start to eat notwithstanding that they were without food for many days. The mongoose was turned golden when he had come into contact with the celestial flowers that had rained and with the particles of barley-powder which that good man gave away. As a result of the gift of that Brāhmiṇ who was firm in his penances, half of the body of the mongoose became golden. But, the remaining had of the body could not be made golden. So, to the Brāhmiṇs he states, 'Hearing of this sacrifice of the Kuru king endued with great wisdom, I come hither with high hopes. I have not, however been made gold. Ye formost of Brāhmiṇs, it is for this that I utter those word, viz., that this sacrifice can by no means compare with (the gift of) the Prastha of powdered barley. With the grains of that Prastha of powdered barley, I am made golden on that occasion. This great sacrifice, however, is not equal to grains. Even this is my opinion."[129]

By means of this story, the epic suggests that not only performing great yajñas with substantial amount of wealth affecting large number of persons is commendable, but even small yajñas like gift in accordance with the capacity of means, satisfying even a single individual, deserves credit. It is not possible for a poor man to perform big yajñas like Rājasuya yajña but he can achieve all the merits of motives. It is evident from the above story that the poor Brāhmiṇ was capable of a great act of self-sacrifice as he was impelled to satisfy the hunger of the poor mendicant by genuine feelings of charity though he himself along with other members of the family was starving.

In the Gītā also, purity of mind is emphasised when Kṛṣṇa declares, "Whosoever offers to me with love a leaf, a flower, a fruit or even water, I appear in person before that disinterested devotee of purified intellect, and delightfully partake of that article offered, by him with love."[130] Purity of motive is also stressed when god Dharma himself states to a Brāhmiṇ that a man who owns a thousand, giving hundred, a man who owns a hundred giving ten, or some one according to his ability giving only a drink of water, all these acts are of the same merit and equally beneficial."[131]

In this connection, Swami Sivananda states, "Purity of motive (Anupadha) is a Sāmānya (general) dharma or common duty of every man. It is the motive that counts in the performance of action. If an action is performed with a selfish motive, it binds a man to the wheel of births and deaths. If it is done with a pure motive in a dis-interested manner, it will purify the heart and lead to the attainment of the final liberation.... Right and wrong are determined not by the objective consequences but by subjective intention of the agent."[132] Thus in the epic, purity of motive is also regarded as an important standard of morality.

(J) Self-realisation as a standard of morality:

In the Hindu ethics, Mokṣa is regarded as the summum bonum of life. It is the highest of the four human goals. It is the goal which each and everyone of us must strive to attain. Salvation or self-realisation is the object of all our ethical endeavours. The epic suggests the way to realise the real self.

In the Śāntiparva, Bhṛgu explains to Bharadvāja the nature of individual self and absolute self thus, "When the Ātman is imprisoned within the body, it is called kṣetrajña (or jīvātman, i. e., personal self). And when the same Ātman is released from these 'Prakṛta' qualities, that is, from the qualities of matter or of the body, it is known as the Paramātman (absolute self)."[133] In the Gītā Kṛṣṇa explains the nature of self as a part of the Absolute. He says, "The jīvātman (soul) in the body is an eternal portion of Myself."[134] It is the real and not an imaginary form of it. It is a limited manifestation of God. The individual self is supposed to be held in bondage when it differentiates itself from Brahman and also when it identifies itself with false-self. Dr. Radhakrishnan puts it in the following manner, "When the ego is lost in a false identification with not-self and its forms, it is bound; but when through the development of proper understanding it realises the true nature of the self and not-self and allows the apparatus produced by the not-self to be illumined completely by the self, then it is freed. This realisation is possible through proper functioning of buddhi or vijñana."[135]

In the Śāntiparva, Viṣṇu describes His own nature to Nārada thus: "He that cannot be seen with eye, touched with the sense of touch, smelt with the sense of scent and that is beyond the ken of the sense of taste; He whom the three attributes of Sattva, Rajas, and Tamas do not touch, who pervades all things and is the one witness of the universe, and who is described as the Soul of the entire universe; He who is not destroyed upon the destruction of the bodies of all created things, who is unborn and unchangeable, freed from all attributes ... who is called by the name of Puruṣa, who is inactive, and who is said to be apprehended by knowledge alone, He into whom the foremost of regenerate persons enter and become emancipated, He who is the eternal Supreme Soul and is known by the name of Vāsudeva."[136] He further states: "I am, O Nārada, the Doer, I am Cause, and I am Effect. I am the sum-total of all living creatures. All living creatures have had their refuge in Me. Let not the thought be thine that thou hast seen the Kṣetrajña. I pervade all things, O Brāhmiṇ, and am the Jīva-soul of all creatures. When the bodies of all creatures, however, are destroyed, I am not destroyed."[137]

In the words of Dr. Radhkrishnan, "When Brahman and Ātman are identified, the highest goal is declared to be unity with the self."[138] For self-realisation, terms like emancipation, deliverance, salvation or Mokṣa have the same meaning. P.

S. Sivaswami Aiyar also opines is this way, "It is not quite easy to identify the Hindu theory of the summum bonum exclusiveness with any of the theories which adopt happiness, perfection or self-realisation as the ultimate end. In so far as the condition of the emancipated souls is described as one of the ineffable bliss, it may be held that happiness is the ultimate end adopted in Hindu ethics. But in so far as, however, as emancipation requires a severe and arduous course of moral discipline, the control of the lower elements of our human nature by the higher and the realisation of the true self or Atman it may be equally correctly said that the summum bonurn of the Hindus involves also perfection and self-realisation."[139]

In the Anaśāsanaparava of the Mahābhārata, Maheśvara mentions that nothing is superior to salvation. Wise men regard this salvation as ceaseless, great and supreme bliss. Learned men and even saints and divine beings regard it as superior to all knowledge. It is fascinating for even Gods and demons as it is eternal, indestructible, unconquerable, everlasting and beneficial. And wise men must achieve it.[140] Salvation has been extolled at many places in the epic. In the Śāntiparva Bhīṣma advises Yudhiṣṭhira to strive for salvation as this world is full of defects and demerits.[141]

It appears from the fact that in the Mahābhārata, the ultimate end of human life as envisaged in orthodox Indian philosophy is not an object of the world but something transempirical or transcendental. The Mahābhārata also subscribes to the Vedantic view that the worldly objects have no permanent value. They are subject to change and decay. Behind this world of change, there is an ultimate reality which is beyond the limits of space and time. It is regarded as immutable, imperishable and all-pervading consciousness. This reality is known as Brahman. The human self is essentially identical with the Universal Self. The Atman and Brahman are one and the same. As Dr. Radhakrishnan puts it, 'The Real is the supracosmic, eternal, spaceless, timeless Brahman who supports this cosmic manifestation in space and time. He is the Universal Spirit, Paramātman, who ensouls the cosmic forms and movements. He is the parameśvara who presides over the individual souls and movements of nature and controls the cosmic becoming. He is also the Puruṣottama, the Supreme Person, whose dual nature is manifested in the evolution of the cosmos. He fills our being, illumines our understanding and sets in motion its hidden springs."[142] The Hindu ethics, as we see, is based on the foundation of the Vedānta Philosophy.

In the Gītā, we find various names[143] given to this highest ideal of life. In the second chapter, this ideal is described as 'Anāmayam' where man is freed from the shackles of birth and attains the blissful supreme state. In the third chapter, it is described as 'Parama' a state when work is done without attachment. It is also called 'Parāṁ Śānti or the Supreme Peace.' It is a state when knowledge is attained and senses are controlled and devoted to spiritual practice. In the fifth chapter, it is described as the state from where there is no return. In the sixth chapter it is also called 'Parāṁgatiṁ' or a state of perfection. Thus it is described in many ways in the Gītā.

The Hindu ethics recognises the threefold paths leading to salvation viz. path of knowledge (Jñāna Mārga), path of action (Karma Mārga) and path of devotion (Bhakti Mārga).

They have been elaborately discussed in the Gītā. Regarding the path of Knowledge in the Śāntiparva, Śuka is told by his father Vyāsa that by knowledge, however, one becomes emancipated.[144] He further remarks, "Through knowledge, however, one becomes transformed into that which is eternal, unmanifest, and immutable. By knowledge one attains to that where there is no occasion for grief, where one becomes freed from both birth and death, where one is not subject to decrepitude, when one transcends the states of conscious existence; there is Brahman which is supreme unmanifest, immutable, ever existent, imperceptible, above the reach of pain, immortal, and transcending destruction."[145] There are numerous verses in the Gītā in praise of jñāna.

Karmayoga is given a more exalted place in the Gītā. The path of action is the better way to attain self-realisation. Kṛṣṇa thus states; 'Knowledge is better than practice (carried on without proper insight), and a meditation is superior to knowledge, and renunciation of the fruit of action is even superior to meditation, for peace immediately follow from renunciation."[146] The Gītā suggests us to perform those duties without any attachment or expectation of the action performed.[147] In the Śāntiparva also, Bhīṣma emphasises it. He says, "Living creatures, by being attached to objects of the senses which are always fraught with evil, become helpless. These high-souled persons, however, who are not attached to them, attain to the highest end."[148] He further observes, "Being pure in speech, and body and freed from pride of tranquill soul and possessed of knowledge, he should lead a life of mendicancy, and pursue happiness without being attached to any worldly object. Again, if attachment be seen to possess the mind in consequences of compassion for creatures, he should, seeing that the universe is the result of acts, show indifference in respect of compassion itself."[149] In the Śāntiparva, Manu states to Bṛhaspati, "It is by liberating oneself from acts that one succeeds on entering into Brahman. The ordinances about acts have flowed from that very end. The ordinances about acts tempt only those whose hearts are not free from desires. By liberating oneself from acts one acquires the highest state."[150]

Besides the paths of Jñānayoga and Karmayoga, the Gītā strongly recommends the path of devotion or Bhakti-Mārga which can deliver the highest goods to all. This path is easier to follow because a person who faithfully devotes himself to the Lord attains Mokṣa not only easily but quickly.[151] It is also stated that even a person who is of a low origin, if he were to take refuge in the Lord, is emancipated.[152]

All these different paths, however, lead to the same goal. As Dr. Radhakrishan puts it, "Whatever be the method we pursue, wisdom, love or service, the end reached is the same, union of the soul with the highest."[153] Thus the epic maintains that Mokṣa or self-realisation is the supreme goal and it prescribes various means to realise it. The identity of the individual self with Brahman is the object of self-realisation. This is of the greatest value in human life. The Upaniṣadic view that empirically pleasant is inferior to transcendentally good is strongly stressed in the epic.

To sum up, though we get verses in the Mahābhārata in support of differet standards of morality in different context, a critical and analytic study reveals that only Mokṣa or liberation is regarded as the ultimate goal of life.

Reference

1. Śānti, 190, 7-9
2. Anu, 111, 37-38.
3. Radhakrishnan, S., Indian Philosophy, P. 505.
4. Vana, 33, 41.
5. Anu, 37, 16.
6. Vana, 206, 90.
7. Śānti, 138, 110, 113, 152-153.
8. Br. Upaniṣad 2, 4; 4,5.
9. Śānti, 167, 9.
10. Udyoga, 39, 71.
11. Śānti, 259, 20, 22.
12. Vana, 209, 5; P. C. Roy, 208.
13. Śānti, 124, 67.
14. Ibid, 361, 9.

15. Gajendragadkar, S. N., Roving Mendicant in the Mahābhārata, journal of the Asiatic Society of Bombay, Vol, 30 1955, pt. I, p. 48.
16. Gītā, 5, 25.
17. Ibid, 2, 4 (Gītā Rahasya).
18. Śānti 167 38.
19. Ibid, 140, 36.
20. Śānti, 190, 9.
21. Sharma, I. C., Ethical Philosophy of India, p.110.
22. Gītā, 6,21.
23. Ibid, 18, 36-39.
24. Śānti, 190, 14.
25. Ibid, 174, 19. 23 & 25.
26. Ibid, 176,4.
27. Vana, 234, 4.
28. Śānti, 139, 63.
29. Ibid, 190, 14.
30. Ibid, 190, 12-13.
31. Ibid, 330, 16; P.C. Roy, 331.
32. Ādi, 75, 50.
33. Śānti, 177, 48.
34. Ibid, 175, 7 & 22.
35. Ibid, 329, 6.
36. Oman, J. C., The Great Epic of India, p. 22.
37. Aiyar, P. S. Sivaswami, Evolution of Hindu Moral Ideals, p. 158.
38. Śānti, 204, 9.
39. Udyoga, 34, 55
40. Śānti, 160, 6-12.
41. Śānti, 174, 45, 49-51.
42. Ibid, 177, 16.
43. Gītā, 2, 55, 58-61.
44. Ibid, 2, 62-63.

45. Ibid, 2, 71.
46. Śānti, 180, 2, 3.
47. Ibid, 194, 18.
48. Ibid, 204, 2-5.
49. Āśva, 14, 9.
50. Hiriyanna, M., Outlines of Indian Philosophy, p. 147.
51. Śānti, 204, 11.
52. Ibid, 248, 2.
53. Ibid, 258, 3-5.
54. Śānti., 218, 1.
55. Tilak, B. G., Gītā Rahasya or Karma-yoga, Vol. I, p. 183.
56. Śānti, 252, 11; Gītā Rahasya, p. 183.
57. Śānti, 250, 3-4.
58. Ibid, 250, 5-6.
59. Maitra, S. K., The Ethics of the Hindus, p. 292.
60. Ādi., 5. 32-34.
61. Ibid, 13, 24. 25-26.
62. Ibid., 195, 7.
63. Ibid., 194, 29.
64. Ibid., 195, 4.
65. Ibid., 195, 15.
66. Śānti, 11, 12.
67. Ibid, 15, 5.
68. Ibid, 26, 27,
69. Śānti, 70, 20.
70. Ibid, 109, 10.
71. Ibid, 90, 19.
72. Vana, 208, 3-4 (P. C. Roy); 209
73. Śānti, 287, 22.
74. Śānti, 259, 4.
75. Ibid, 90, 5.
76. Tilak, B. G., Gītā Rahasys p. 90-91

77. Nivedita. Sister, Preface, Religion and Dharma.
78. Dasgupta, Surama, Development of Moral Philosophy in India p. 20.
79. Ibid.
80. Ibid., p. 22,
81. Valavalkar, Pandharinath H., Hindu Social Institutions, p. 327-328
82. Śānti, 57, 15.
83. Aurobindo, Vyāsa & Vālmiki, p. 63.
84. Śānti, 15, 53.
85. Gītā 19, 45.
86. Ibid 18, 46.
87. Ibid. 5, 31.
88. Ibia, 18, 47.
89. Udyoga, 40, 12,
90. Gītā, 3, 19.
91. Gītā,17, 11
92. Vana, 31, 2-5.
93. Śānti, l5, 34.
94. Ibid, 15, 43.
95. Ibid, 15, 5.
96. Ibid, 15, 25.
97. Śānti, 15, 2.
98. Abhyankar, Vasudev Shastri, Sarva-Darsana Saṁgraha, Cārvākadarsana, p, 7.
99. Maitra, S.k. The Ethics of the Hindus, p. 316.
100. Sānti, 59, 29-89.
101. Ibid, 59, 15.
102. Anu, 141, 65.
103. Śānti, 68, 28.
104. Maitra, S. K. The Ethies of the Hindus, p. 320.
105. Ibid, b. 315.
106. Śānti, 15, 20.

107. Ibid, 134, 20.
108. Śānti, 134, 6-7.
109. Ibid, 134, 8.
110. Sabhā, 69, 15.
111. Śānti, 133, 4.
112. Udyoga, 37, 52-55.
113. Śāntī, 134, 5.
114. Santa, 134, 5.
115. Vana, 313, 115.
116. Ibid., 313, 117.
117. Śalya, 61-68.
118. Vana, 197, 3-23. P. C. Roy, 196.
119. Ibid, 198, 26.
120. Gītā, 3. 21.
121. Gītā, 3, 2g.
122. Mishra, H. N., Moral Philosophy, Green & Gītā, p. 152.
123. Śānti, 35, 48.; Anu, 141, 65.
124. Ibid, 262, 19 & 21.
125. Ibid, 262, 36.
126. Ayodhyā, XXI, 36.
127. Maitra, S. K., The Ethies of the Hindus, p. 313.
128. Āśva, 90, 7.
129. Ibid, 90. 115.
130. Gītā, 9, 26.
131. Āśva, 90, 96.
132. Swami Sivanada, Ethical Teaching, p. 9.
133. Śānti, 187, 13.
134. Gītā, 15, 7.
135. Radhakrishnan, Bhagavadgītā, p. 45.
136. Śānti, 330, 21-25.
137. Śānti, 339, 42-13, 47-48.
138. Radhakrishnan, S., Principal Upanisads, p. 117.

139. Aiyar, P. S. Sivaswami, Evolution of Hindu Moral Ideals, p. 153.
140. Anu, 145, (p. 6008, G. P.)
141. Śānti, 174, 5.
142. Radhakrishnan, S., The Bhagavadgītā, p. 27.
143. Gītā, 2, 51; 3. 19; 4. 39; 4. 17; 16, 23.
144. Śānti, 241, 7.
145. Ibid, 241, 8.
146. Gītā, 12, 12.
147. Ibid, 2, 47.
148. Śānti, 215, 1.
149. Śānti, 215, 3, 4.
150. Ibid, 201, 13.
151. Gītā, 12, 7.
152. Ibid, 9, 32.
153. Radhakrishnan, S., Indian Philosophy, vol. 1. p. 574.

6

Summary and Conclusion

The ethics of the Hindus is essentially Dharma-centric. When Dharma is described as a code of conduct which holds people together in integrating individual's character, organising society and assuring political stability by performing Vedic rituals, observing duties of the Dharmaśāstras and following the paths trodden by pious and learned men leading to prosperity (Abhyudaya) and salvation (Niḥśreyasa) of the individual, it includes all values within its fold social and individual, political and philosophical, religions and legal. It is used in such a broad sense that it becomes all-comprehensive. The elements of social and individual ethics come under Varṇśāramadharma. Generally speaking, Varṇadharmas are social duties, while Āśramadharmas are personal duties. Though, they cover two different groups of duties, they may be subsumed under the common category of Dharma. The political ethics also comes under Dharma. The moral duties meant for the king and the subject have been dealt with in the epic under the section of Rājadharmānuśāsanaparva. These ethical codes have been laid down with a view to helping the Individual and communities in achieving their ends. The primary objective of the epic is to ensure social good along with individual good in this life and the next. In short, the epic promulgates such ethical principles as are conducive not only to the well-being of the individual and society on this earth but also to the well-being of all living creatures. Dr. B. G.

Gokhale rightly remarks, "The range of thought encompassed by the concept of Dharma, thus, is most comprehensive... It has so completely permeated Indian thinking and manifested itself so repeatedly and continuously in action that it has almost become the central point of all thoughts on religion and metaphysics, ethics and polity, law and filial behaviour. One of the meanings of the term Dharma is quality or attitude or characteristic and through its universality the concept of Dharma has become a norm for all human action in India."[1]

The ethics of the Hindus is relative. It is flexible and adaptable. Its main aim is to serve the purpose of bringing social equilibrium, social stability with the all-round personality development of the individual. In this connection, P. N. Prabhu states that the recognition of the role of time and region in the formation of Dharma is an indication of an awareness that the concept of Dharma was not a rigid concept but a flexible, modifiable and dynamic principle related to the exigencies of time, place and human needs.[2] In this regard, Dr. Gokhale observes, "What the concepts of Kāla and Deśa imply is that given the difference in outlooks and attitudes of different periods and times the details of a scheme of human conduct be the same at all times and in all places. This prevented the concept of Dharma from becoming a stratified idea by leaving the possibility, open for change in its institutionalized character."[3] With regard to social ethics, distinct rights and duties have been enlisted for all the classes yet there is room for exceptions. In extraordinary times, these duties have been allowed to change with varying situations and circumstances. This is the most liberal conception of Dharma Swami Nikhilanand justifies the relative nature of Dharma. And takes absolute Dharma as the cause of injustice. He says, "Hinduism emphasises the relative nature of Dharma, and does not recognise absolute good or evil: evil may be described as what is less good. One cannot stipulate what is absolutely good or evil for all Men at all times. The attempt to do so, and to judge all people, by a single concept of dharma or to impose upon all a single idea of rightness, has been the cause of much injustice to humanity."[4]

The lack of such accommodating or relative ethics is noticed in later periods. After the epic era, the Varṇadharma took a rigid shape, and became stereotype and inflexible.

The liberal character of the ethics of the Hindus is amply borne out by the prevalence of 'Niyoga', 'Pāṇḍu and Dhṛtarāśṭra were born by Niyoga. Kuntī and Mādri produced children by Niyoga. There are instances in the epic which show that children were born even of unmarried mothers. Satyavati gave birth to Vyāsa by sage Parāśara and Kuntī to Karṇa before their marriages. There are passages in the epic which testify to free sex relations. In Mādra-deśa and the country of the Bahikās and also in Anga, the tradition of promiscuity was prevslent.[5] The sex ethics was sometimes so liberal that a polluted woman was accepted as cleansed after her menstrual flow. Vyāsa himself states, "They (Women) are cleansed by their menstrual course like a metallic plate that is scoured with ashes."[6]

The pragmatic nature of ethics in the epic is also evidenced by the fact that it permits all classes to fight when any danger is apprehended from outside or inside. The fixed duties of the four classes were not always insisted upon with rigour. Class-duty was determined not only by birth but also by quality and action. It was functional, and not structural.

Now-a-days there is a fashion to criticise the class system. The vague and confusing ideas about class are responsible for it. People generally identify ancient class system with modern caste system. But the present caste system is only the ghost of the class system. As Mahadev Desai observes, "Much of the criticism is directed against which is just a shadow of what existed ages ago. There was a system which existed in ages gone by which served the then existing social organism magnificently which was elastic and hence made it possible for a number of different groups of the same race and served races to live together in amity and peace: What we see today is its travesty, a fossil formed out of the incrustations of customs and practices of several centuries."[7] When we criticise the caste system, we criticise the distorted form of class system and not the class system as such which existed at the time of the epic. Such a criticism is based on misconception. The class system had its own purposes for which it was brought into existence. Just contrary to it, the caste system was developed on the line of self-interest of some people or groups of people. It had its own motives for which it came into existence. Radhakrishnan remarks in this connection that caste-system is a degeneration of the class idea.[8]

The class system is rooted in organic conception of society. Each class was supposed to work for the betterment of the organism and also for its own preservation. The important point underlying this class system was the division of labour. The whole social service was divided into four main groups of services and each group was assigned to a group of persons for their performances. However, it is worth mentioning here that particular groups were not entrusted to perform different sets of services arbitrarily but on the basis of hereditary traits of character, aptitude and disposition. The other marked feature was that services were done very efficiently and satisfactorily. The unity of society was of prime necessity. In spite of the differences in duties and rights, there was no class-hatred. There was mutual understanding and cooperation among people. No class was looked upon with contempt. Duties were changeable in accordance with the growing needs of society. According to Udaibhan Singhji, this type of class system can be noticed in all societies and at all times. It was rather obligatory on the part of both society and the individual to divide services into different parts for the regular functioning of society. He observes: "Of this, I am certain that no country of population, anywhere, can ever hope to be logically balanced with consistent happily results, in human society if it is not divided correctly in four essential divisions at the service of the whole, namely, thoroughly honest and far-sighted counsellors, brave and loyal soldiers, shrewd economists and traders, hard working and willing labourers. Such proportioned societies have done wonders in the past and will, always, be capable of turning real deserts into smiling habitations for mankind for the greatest good of human society."[9] According to Prof. J. S. Mackenzie, such type of division of labour is also found in Germany. Prof. Mackenzie in an article on 'The present look in Social Philosophy', writes, "In the life of a nation, it seems possible to make a clear distinction between three important forms of activity-the cultural, the economic, and the legal or political. They form the bases for three higher castes of India, and they are commonly recognised in Germany as the Lehrstand, the Wehrstand, and the Nhrastrand' (Some German writers speak of a fourth, the Verkerstand) the workmen, corresponding to the Shudras caste."[10] Even Swami Vivekanand does not take it otherwise and treats it as the stepping stone to civilization, making one rise higher and higher in proportion to one's learning and culture.[11]

On the one hand, we find class system as the binding force of social integration, while on the other, caste system as it is today is the root cause of social disintegration. K. M. Panikkar finds this caste-system as an obstacle in the development of any common social feeling.[12] Dharma Theethaji regards it as a part of mental constitution of the Hindus. For him, there is no aspect of the nation's life which has not been vitiated, no institution which has not been tarnished, no saint and martyr who has not been victimised by caste.[13] He further holds it responsible as a factor for dividing the Hindus. To him, the caste divisions not only make the Hindu society a house divided against itself, but also a community which, is up in arms against all other communities and against whom all other communities are up in arms.[14] He does not even hesitate in calling the Hindu social system undemocratic, anti-national and imperialistic.[15] Undoubtedly, we find today that the castes have become antagonistic instead of being complementary and helpful to one another. Even in one caste, there are many sub-castes and they often fight among themselves. Society as a whole suffers on account of such inner conflicts. The perfect and proper growth of the personality of individuals is impossible in the environment of class-hatred. These days caste consideration plays an important role in politics too. Some politicians use caste feeling for their political gain destroying the social harmony and creating ill will in society. The lack of mutual co-operation and the rise of disruptive forces are eating into the vitals of the social organism and precipitating economic, political and moral crises.

Now a question arises in this connection: whether in present times this class system can improve the social morality of the people? Can this caste system be reorganised on the lines of ancient class system? Should class system be revived? The answer of all these questions will be in the negative. The actual revival of this Varṇa system is practically impossible. The political power is being shifted from the hands of higher to the lower classes. Every citizen has equal right to elect a government. The transfer of political power has provided the masses with a power to destroy the social institutions based on privilege or on hereditary equality. It cannot allow the revival of any classification on the basis of class system. The present constitution of India provides equal opportunities to all, irrespective of one's age, class, sex etc.[16] Thus the Indian Constitution of today does not take any cognizance of the class system. The state always provides laws to guarantee fundamental rights of the individual. The Nepalese Constitution too does not permit any class distinctions and provides guarantee for equal opportunity to all irrespective of one's class and creed etc.[17] Another factor that stands in the way of the revival of the class system in the modern days, is the admixture of vocations. Today, there is no particular group doing a particular job in society. Almost all professions seem to have been taken up by people of all castes. It is necessary for the technical and industrial development of society, that all people are equal to do all works in society. A division of people based on their professions, will not only give rise to complications, but will also break the social unity. The present day communistic tendency is not in favour of class distinction in society. Communism envisages a classless society. In the present-set-up of things, no individual or group likes to be dominated by another. Thus it does not seem possible to revive the ancient class system today.

In this connection, it may not be out of place to state that many modern thinkers seem to have entertained different and opposing views regarding the revival of the class system. On the conclusion of his book, K. M. Panikkar remarks, "The theory of Hindu social life does not accept the idea of a community for it is based on division not on unity."[18] He wants unceasing activities directed towards the development of the physical, moral and intellectual life of the people as a whole. He does not want class system to be the basic principle of social integration.[19] In this regard, Ketkar says, "The doctrine of four varṇas, if properly understood, is a very healthy doctrine for any people. This doctrine does not support the caste-system but is antagonistic to it. When the Brāhmiṇs insisted on this doctrine, in most cases their attempts were not blameworthy. Still it is necessary to change that doctrine now."[20] Mahatma Gandhi also wants this Varṇāśṛamadharma to be corrected.

He does not, however, want its destruction altogether. He observes, "Today Varṇāśramadharma and Hinduism are misrepresented and denied by its, votaries. The remedy is not destruction, but correction:"[21] Rabindra Nath Tagore wants it to go, but he wants a new system. In the words of Brij Gopal Tiwari, 'He (Tagore) believes that the historic function of the caste-system was to realise the ideal of peace and amity, so that people of various races, traditions and occupations could live together like members of one family. But the caste system has out-lived its usefulness. So, it must be discarded and a new system, based on the same principle of racial and cultural harmony must be evolved in its place."[22] Udaibhan Singhji thinks that all the evils of the Hindu society will be recued if all sub-castes are merged into the four.[23]

No doubt, the class system had its significance for the social life of the ancient periods. It may be admitted that it was rather essential to regulate the then existing social morality of the people. So the usefulness and moral significance of the class system in those times cannot be denied. But due to the evolution of a higher and altogether different type of society which has become enormously big and complex today, old framework of class system will no longer suit the purpose. Today, a father can be a farmer while his son may be a soldier or an educationist. Thus, the Varṇāśamadharmas of the epic will not fit in modern set-up of things.

The Hindu ethics furnishes enough contributions in the field of individual morality. The stage system, as we find in the epic, has still its values for our life. It is not dogmatic but based on scientific and practical outlook of ancient seers. When we observe this system as a whole, we find that it is fully in accordance with the physico-psychical set-up of the man. The divisions of life into Brahmacaryāśrama, Gṛhasthāśramā, Vānaprasthāśrama and Saṁnyāsāśrama still hold good in this era of science and technology but of course in a different form. Boys and girls are sent to their schools, colleges and universities for study in the first part of their lives. They enter family life after they complete their education. The first stage is supposed to be the most effective for the purpose of study and learning. The brain at an early stage functions sharply and grasps things promptly and easily. The life of the householder is also noticed in all societies in different capacities as a farmer, businessman, teacher or doctor. Such a life continues till men become old and physically unable to work. This stage of retirement roughly corresponds to the third stage viz. the life of the hermit. Though we find important differences between the ancient life of the hermit and present retired life. People no longer go to lead Vānaprasthya life in solitude as a stepping stone to Saṁnyāsāśrama. However, in the present social set-up also, there is a tendency in retired men to lead a life of retirement in a spirit of detachment from household affairs. In this form, even the last two stages are traceable to some extent in our lives. The first āśrama is the stage of learning, the second is that of action the third is of spiritual thinking and the fourth is of realisation. Mahatma Gandhi also appreciates this āśrama system when he says, "Thus there is the contribution of the four ashramas, again a unique contribution. There is nothing like it in the whole world. The Catholics have the order of celibates corresponding to Brahmacāris, but not as an institution, whereas in India every body had to go through the first ashrama. What a grand conception it was."[24]

General Dharmas which occupy a very important place in Hindu ethics are still valuable in the present day morality. They are more necessary at present than Varṇāśramadharmas. We have maintained in the foregoing pages that usually, they are primary and compulsory for all irrespective of their class and stage. We have described these Dharmas earlier. They include Harmlessness, Truthfulness, Non-anger, Austerity, Absence of pride, Not to final faults with others, Modesty,

Simplicity, Charity, Good manners, Tolerance, Tranquillity, Freedom from greed, etc. They possess perennial value and uplift the moral tone of society.

The evils existing in the present society are mostly due to our departure from Dharma. It cannot be denied that we are living in an age of moral crisis. If we reinstate Dharmas in social, economic and political fields, the world can become a better place to live in. Dharma is a panacea for the troubles we are facing today. If the ethical teachings of the, great epic are properly understood and sincerely practised, they will certainly help us in improving the tone of our national and international morality. Every community, if it abides by Dharma, every individual if he follows Svadharma will contribute to the moral up lift of society which will function in an orderly fashion and reach the cultural, religious, political and moral height again. The ethics preached in the Mahābhārata are still applicable and can help us in establishing the kingdom of morality.

The popular form of the government in the epic period was Kingship, but the interest of the public was considered as a sacred trust. The Kingship was the custodian of law, order, justice and social good. The Government was not OF THE PEOPLE, and BY THE PEOPLE, but it was always and necessarily FOR THE PEOPLE. Swami Vivekanand appreciates very much the political morality and specially war ethics as found in the epic. He says, "The most curious thing was the code of war of the days; as soon as the battle for the lay ceased and evening came, the opposing parties were good friends, even going to each other's tent, however when the morning came, again they proceeded to fight each other, That was the strange trait the Hindu carried down to the time of the Mohammedan invasions."[25] The war-mongers of today who destroy innocent citizens by atom bombs should take lesson from the canons of just war in the Mahābhārata which enjoined that "A man on horseback must not strike one on foot; must not poison the weapon, must not vanquish the enemy in any unequal fight, or by dishonesty, and must never take undue advantages of another, and so on. If any one deviated from these rules he would be covered with the dishonours and shunned, the kshatriyas were trained in the way."[26] Even enemies were treated with humane considerations. To quote Swami again, "And the foreign invasion came from central Asia, the Hindus treated the invaders in the self-same way. They defeated several times, and on as many occasions sent them back to their homes with presents, etc. The code laid down was that they must not usurp anybody's country; and when a man is beaten, he must be sent back to his country with due regard to his position,"[27]

Dharma and particularly Rājadharma was the guiding principle of the political morality in the epic era. For the betterment and benefit of both rule and the ruled, Dharma determines the mutual rights and duties of both the sides. It is the obligation of the king to maintain the propriety of behaviour and relation in accordance with Dharma by administering justice to restore social equilibrium. If the ruler's behaviour is not in accordance with Dharma, his government cannot function for a long time. Similarly, if the people do not behave in accordance with Dharma they will surely come to grief. So Dharma is essential for the well-being of both the ruler and the people.

In the Mahābhārata, we find stress on human endeavours in shaping individual's character. Sometimes emphasis is also laid upon Fate. Ultimately the epic asks men not to depend upon Fate. The Fate of the Individual is a subject of his will. By performing actions in accordance with Dharma we can very easily undo the effects of past deeds which have been stored as Destiny and may succeed in framing a few bright future.

We have discussed various standards of morality as found in the epic. The teleological standard and specially self-relisation, or perfection as the goal is regarded as the supreme standard. It is mentioned repeatedly that out of the four ends - salvation has been extolled as the ultimate end of life. Such moral standards as social good, purity of motives, behaviour of great men, duty, law, tradition and custom etc. help us in achieving the supreme end. Dharma is given much importance in the epic because it is conducive to the attainment of perfection of individual and social planes of life.

The different ethical elements in the Hindu ethics move round the central concept of Dharma which is the all-embracing concept in the epic. The Hindu ethics is out and out Dharma-centric. In short, the great epic exhorts the practice of virtue on the part of the individual and community for their material, moral and spiritual well-being. The central message of the Mahābhārata in the light of which we can reorient our outlook and reconstruct our social life, can be summed up in the well-known maxim- "Yato dharmastato jayaḥ"[28], i.e, where there is Dharma, there is triumph.

To accept, 'Where there is Dharma, there is triumph', means that it is Duty that prevails ultimately. Duty and Right are relative concepts, as any Duty has its corresponding Right. For example, of not to kill any body, is one's Duty, it suggests that not to be killed is his Right. Hence, Duty is primary. Sadly, it is lacking everywhere in our personal, social and political lives today. Any nation or any culture must cultivate the culture of duty not only towards society and nation but also towards human civilization and environment in order to breathe in to survive.

Finally, in order to explain the complex nature of Duty, we have to refer back to the event that determined the main course of the story. These happenings threw ample light over the future course of the story. In the Sabhā Parva, the Kauravas, who were determined not to allow the Pāndavas to acquire the throne, wanted them to forfeit their claim by making them lose the game of dice deceitfully. Hence, in the arranged game they asked Yudhiṣthira, the eldest brother to stake himself, who lost it to become their slave. In course of the game, he not only lost his four younger brothers but also his wife, Draupadī. She was the common wife of the five Pāndavas. Duḥśāsana, the second brother of Duryodhana dragged her to the court calling her their slave or maidservant. Draupadī, being duly married to the Pāndavas and a respectable member of the royal family, raised an important question to the king and the respected personalities of the clan and other learned men assembled there to confirm whether she had really become their slave. The question involved was: Yudhiṣthira, after losing the game and becoming a slave, was he right to stake their common wife like an object? She questions: where has the Dharma of kings gone today?

Bhīṣma, however, tries to answer the question in the context of 'Might is Right' as a standard of morality (Chapter-5) indirectly. He seems to avoid his commitment on the question by stating that he does not want to evaluate the question, as the nature of Dharma is subtle and cites the example of old and the knower of Dharma Droṇacārya, who is sitting bowing his head like a lifeless being. He states further that Yudhiṣṭhira who is the authentic person to reply can answer the question and he should decide whether she has become a slave or not (Chapter-79). Interestingly, Bhīṣma praises Draupadī for her adherence to Dharma and for not deviating from the path of Dharma at this most critical situation. Perhaps, he was suggesting indirectly that as a reward, she should be rescued and actually Kṛṣṇa rescues her. He also foretells that due to gross greed and infatuation, the destruction of this clan appears imminent and that too actually happens, when all members of the family are killed in the war along with Acarya (Guru) Droṇa, Kripācārya and himself. An unanswered question remains in this connection: Why did Bhīśma, who was known for his vow of not to claim for the throne and not to marry and practice celibacy throughout his life to forfeit the claim of his offspring too for the sake of the pleasure of his father, not follow his Dharma by standing firm against the greedy and unjust Dhṛtarāṣṭrā and his sons to avoid the deadliest war? Is the subtle nature of Dharma responsible for all that happened?

Reference

1. Gokhale, B. G., Indian Thought through the Ages, p. 48.
2. Pradhu, P. N., Hindu Social Organisation 1. 74.
3. Gokhale, B. G., Indian Though Through the Ages, p. 42.
4. Nikhilanand, Swami, Hinduism, p. 71.
5. Karṇa, 28 & 30; Cri, Edi, 40, 44 & 45.
6. Śānti, 35, 30.
7. Desai, Mahadev, The Gospel of Selfless Action of the Gītā according to Gandhi, p. 102.
8. Radhakrishnan, S., Eastern Religion and Western Thought, p. 378.
9. Singhiji, Udaibhan, Eastern Light of Sanatana Culture, p. 273-274.
10. Das, Bhagvan, The Science of Religion of Sanatana Vaidika Dharma, p. 100; The Journal of Philosophical Studies, Vol, I, No. I, January, 1926.
11. Vivekanand; Swami, The complete Work, Vol, v. p. 439.
12. Panikkar, K. M. Hindu Society at Cross Roads, p. 12.
13. Theerthaji, Dharma, The Menace of Hindu Imperialism; p. 220.
14. Ibid., p. 227
15. Ibid., p. 314.
16. Art. 15 (1)
17. Art. 18, 2.

18. Panikkar, K. M., Hindu Society at Cross Roads, p. 94.
19. Ibid., p. 95,
20. Ketar., S. V., An Essay on Hinduism, p. XXV.
21. Mahatma Gandhi, Young India, November 24, 1927.
22. Tiwari, Brij Gopal, Secularism and Materialism in Modern India, p. 65.
23. Singhji, Udaibhan, Eastern Light of Sanatana Culture, p. 281
24. Mahatma, Gandhi, "Young India, November, 1926.
25. Vivekanand, The Complete Work, vol. IV, p.89.
26. Ibid,
27. Ibid,
28. Bhīśma, 2, 14; 21, 11.

Bibliography

Sources

The Malābhārāta: P. C. Roy, 12 Vols. English Translation.:

The Malābhārāta: critical editions, Bhandarkar Oriental Research Institute, Poona.

The Malābhārāta: Gita Prass, Gorakhpur, Hindi and Sanskrit Version.

The Malābhārāta: R. S. Sharma, Hindi & Sanskrit Version.

Secondary Books

Agarwal, Basudeo Saran: Bhārata Sāvitrī, 1st and IInd Vols., Ist edition, 1964-65.

Aiyangar, K.V. Rangaswami: Some Aspects of the Hindu View of Life according to Dharmaśāstra, Baroda University, 1952

Aiyangar, Rangaswarni: Indian Heritage, Vol. III, 2nd edi. 1961.

Altekar, A. S. State and Government in Ancient India, 2nd edi., 1965.

Atreya, B. L.: Bhartīya Nīti Śāstra Kā Itihāsa, 1st edi., 1965.

Aurobindo: Vyāsa and Valmīki. 1st edi., 1956.

Bandhopadyaya, Narayan Chandra: Development of Hindu Polity & Political Theories, Calcutta, 1927.

Banerjee, Nekunja Vihari,: Glimpses of Indian wisdom, Munshiram Manoharlal, New Delhi. 1972.

Bentham, Jeremy: Principles of Morals & Legislation, ; Oxford, 1823.

Besant, Annie: Hindu ideals, Adyar, 1965.

Besant, Annie: Indian Ideals in Education, Religion and Philosophy, 1965.

Besant, Annie: The Universal Text book of Religion & Morals. 3rd edi. 1962.

Bhandarkar, D. R.: Some Aspects of Ancient Hindu polity, 2nd edi., 1953.

Bhandarkar, D. R.: Lectures on the Ancient History of India, University of Calcutta, 1919.

Bhattacharya, Sukhamaya: Mahābhārata Kṛṣṇa Samāja, Allahabad, 1966. Translated by Puspa Jain.

Bhatta, Pandit Rameshwar: Manu Smṛti, 2nd edi., 1922.

Barth, A.: The Religion of India, London, 1882.

Bradley, F. H.: Ethical Studies, 2nd edi., 1927.

Broad, C. D.: Five Types of Ethical theory, London, 6th edi., 1951.

Buch, Maganlal Amritlal: The Principals of Hindu Ethics, Paroda, 1921.

Buch, Maganlal Amritlal: The Spirit of Ancient Hindu Culture, Baroda, 1921.

Chatterji, Satischandra & Dutta, D. M.: An Introduction to Indian Philosophy, 6th edi., 1960.

Choudhary, Nirad, C. Hinduism, oxford university press, New york, 1979.

Colebroke, Hanry Thomas: Essays on the Religion & Philosophy of the Hindus, London, 1858.

Das, Bhagvan: The Science of Social Organism or The Laws of Manu, Vol. 1 & III, 2nd edi., Benaras, 1948.

Das, Bhagvan: The Science of Religion or Sanatana Vaidika Religion, 2nd edi., Benaras, 1948,

Dasgupta, Rama Prasad: A Study in Hindu and Eurorean Political System, Calcutta, 1958

Dasgupta, Surama: Development of Moral Philosophy in India, 1st edi., 1964.

Desai, Mahadev: The Gospel of Selfless action or the Gita according to Gandhi, Ahmadabar, 4th edi., 1956.

Dial Sarab.: A Handbook on Morals and Ethics. Ambala Cantt., 1962.

Dikshitar, V. R. Ramachandra: Hindu Ministrative Institutions, Madras, 7931.

Dixit, V.V.: Relation of the Epics to the Brāhmana Literature, Poona, 1956.

Drekmeir, Charles: Kingship and Community in Early India, Bombay, 1962.

Dutt, N. K.: Origin end Growth (development) of Caste in India, 1931.

Dutta, Romesh Chandra: The Early Hindu Civilization. 4th edi, Calcutta, 1963.

Dutta, Romesh Chandra: A History of Civilization of Ancient India, Vol. I. Calcutta, 1889. (Revised in two Vol., 1893).

Emile, Senart: Caste in India, the Facts and the System, Trans. by D. Ross, London.

Farquhar, John Nieol: The Crown of Hinduism, Oxford University Press, 1915.

Farquhar, John Nieol: A Primer of Hinduism, London, 1912.

Farquhar: An Outline of the Religious Literature of India, Oxford, 1920.

Farquhar: A Primer of Hinduism, London, 1912.

Foulder, R.: The Principles of Moral and Political Philosophy, 9th edi., London, 1893.

Gandhi, M. K.: Hindu Dharma, Ahmadabad, 1950.

Gandhi, M. K.: Gita the Mother, edi. by Jag Pravesh Chandra, 4th edi., 1946, Lahore.

Ghosh, Batakrishna: Hindu Ideal of Life, Calcutta, 1949.

Ghosal, U.N. A History of Indian Political Ideas, Oxford University Press, 1959.

Ghurye, G.S.: Caste, Class and Occupation, Bombay,: 1961.

Ghurye, G.S.: Caste and Race in India, 1932.

Gokhale, B.G.: Indian. Thought Through the Ages, Asia Publishing House, Bombay, 1961.

Hari Haran, M.: Hinduism and its Rationalism, Madras, 1961.

Hayavadana: Indian Caste System, Bangalore, 1932.

Hellock, James: Ethical Studies, Personal, Social and Religious, Madras, 1959.

Hiriyanna, M.: Out Lines of Indian Philosophy, London, 3rd edi., 1956.

Holderness, T. W.: Peoples and Problems of India, London, 1920.

Hopkins, E. W.: Ethics of India, U.S.A., 1924.

Hopkins, E. W.: The Mutual Relations of the Four Castes, Leipzing, 1881.

Hopkins, E. W.: Legends of India, New Hoven, 1928.

Hopkins, E. W.: The Great Epic of India, its Character and Origin, New York, 1909.

Hopkins, E. W.: The Religions of India, London, 1896.

Hutton, J. H.: Caste in India, its Nature, Function & Origin, Oxford University Press, 3rd edi., 1961.

lyer, K. Balasubramania: Yaksha Prshna, Bhartiya Vidya Bhavan, 1st edi., Bombay, 1953.

Jayaswal, K. P.: Hindu Polity, 3rd edi., Bangalore, 1955.

Joad, C.E.M.: Ethics of Common Sense,

Kapadia, K. M.: Hindu Kingship, Bombay, 1941.

Kane, P.V.: History of Dharmaśāstra, Vol-I & Vol-II, Part I, B. O. R. I. Poona, 1941.

Ketkar, Shridhar V.: The History of Caste in India, 1st Vol. New York,. 1909.

Ketkar, Shridhar V.: History of Caste in India, 2nd Vol. London, 1911.

Keith, A. B.: History of Sanskrit Literature, 1947.

MAC Donell, A. A.: A History of Sanskrit Literature, London, 1925.

MAC Donell, A. A.: India's Past, Oxford, 1927.

Macflee, John Mandevelle: Myths & Legends of India, Edinburh, 1924.

Mahadevan, T. M. P.: Outlines of Hinduism, Bombay, 2nd edi. 1960.

Maitra, A. C.: Elements of Morals, Cuttak, 1912.

Maitra, S. K.: The Ethics of the Hindus, 3rd edi., 1963 Calcutta.

Majumdar, R. C.: Ancient India.

Majumdar, R. C.: Corporate Lift in Ancient India,

Mazumdar, A. K.: Outlines of Moral Philosophy, Calcutta, 1915.

Mazumdar, J. C.: Ethics of the Mahābhārata, Calcutta, 1953.

Mckenzie, J.: Hindu Ethics, England, 1922.

Mill, J. S.; Utilitarianism, Liberty & Repressntative Government, 1960.

Mishra, H. N.: Moral Philosophy, Green & Gīta, Kanpur.

Mookerji, Radha Kumud: Ancient Indian Education, London, 1947.

Mookerji, Radha Kumud: Men and Thought in Ancient London.

Mookerji, Radha Kumud: Hindu Civilization, Great Britain, 1st edi., 1636.

Motwani Kewal: Mann A Study of Hindu Social Theory, Madras, 1934 (enlarged edi.)

Muir, J.: Maxims & Sentiments from the Mahābhārata, Edinburgh, 1876.

Mukerjee, Radhakamal: The Indian Scheme of Life, Bombay, 1st edi., 1951.

Mullick, P. N.: The Mahābhārata, as it was, is and shall be Ist edi., 1934, Calcutta.

Narang, Gokul Chand: Rea Hinduism. London, Ist edi., 1947.

Nikhilanand, Swami: Hinduism; Its meaning for the Liberation of the Spirit, New York, 1958.

Nivedita, Sister: Religion & Dharma, 1st edi. 1952.

OMen, J. C.: The Great Epic of India, New York, 1894.

Prasad, Narmadeshwar: The Myth of the Caste System, Patna, 1957.

Pusalkar, A. D.: Studies in Epic & Puranas of India, Bhartiya Vidya Bhawan, 1955.

Paley, William: The Principles of Moral and Political Philosophy, London new edi., 1928.

Panday, Manubhai C.: Intelligent Man's guide to Indian philosophy, Bombay, 1935.

Panikkar, K.M.: Hindu society at cross mads, Asia publishing house, Bombay, 1st edi., 1955.

Prasad, Beni: State in Ancient India, Allahabad, 1928.

Radhakrishnan, S.: Indian philosophy, two Vols., Ist. edi, 1929.

Radhakrishnan, S.: The Hindu View of Life, Great Britain, 7th edi., 1948.

Radhakrishnan, S.: (edi. by): History of Philosophy: Eastern and western, 2nd edi., 1957.

Radhakrishnan, S.: Bhagavadgītā, London,. 2nd edi., 1949.

Radhakrishnan, S.: Society and Religion, London, 1947.

Radhakrishnan, S.: Eastern Religion and western thought, Oxford university press, 2nd edi. 1940.

Rajagopalachari, C.: Mahābhārata, Bhartiya vidya Bhawan, Bombay 7th edi., 1962.

Ray, Gulab: Karttvya Śastra, saka year, 1976.

Renou, Louis: Hinduism, New york, 1662.

Roger. A.P. Reginald: A short History of Ethics (Greek & modern), London, 1930.

Russell, Bertrand: Human society in ethics and Politics, Lund, 1934.

Saltore, B. Anand: Ancient Indian political thought and Institution, Calcutta, 1963.

Sarkar, Benoy Kumar: The foke ement in Hindu Culture, London, 1917.

Sarkar, Benoy Kumar: Creative India, Lahore, 1937.

Sarkar, Kishorilal: The Hindu system of Science Calcutta,1898.

Sarasvati, Chandra Sekharandra: The Sanatan Dharma, or the Hindu, View of life, Madras, 1946.

Sastri, K.S. Ramaswami: A Mahābhārata Primer, Tirupati, 1950.

Saunders, Kenneth James: The Ideals of East and West, Cambridge. 1934.

Sehweitzer, Albert: Indian Thought and its development, London, 1951.

Scott, Roland Waldeck: Social Ethics in modern Hinduism, Calcutta, 1953.

Sen, K.M.: Hinduism, 1st edi., 1961 (Benguin books).

Sharma C.D.: A Critical Survey of Indian Philosophy, 1st edi., London, 1960.

Sharma, D.S. : Hinduism Through the Ages, 2nd edi., 1962, Bombay.

Sharma, I.C.: Ethical Philosophy of India.

Sharma, Uma Sankar: Sarva Darśana Saṁgraha (Translated), 1st edi., 1964.

Singh, Thakur Rajendra: The Great War of Ancient India, its cause, its issuse, its lesson, Allahabad, 1915.

Singhji, Udaibhan: Fastern Light of Sanatana Culture, Calcutta, 1916.

Sivaswamy Aiyar, P.S-: Evolution of Hindu Moral Ideals, Calcutta. 1935.

Srinivaschari, A.M.: 'Mahābhārata (in abridged form), 1st edi., Madras, 1935.

Stephen, Sir Leslie: Social Rights and Duties, London, 1896.

Sukathankar, V.S.: On the Meaning of the Mahābhārata,

Swami Dharma Theerthji: The Menace of Hindu Imperialism, Maharaj, Lahore. 1941.

Swami Gananada: Wisdom of Sanatan Dharma, Madras.

Swami, Sivananda, Etical Teachings, reshikash, 2nd .edi. 1962.

Swami, Ganauanda: Wisdom of Sanatan Dharma, Madras, (year not given).

Swami Sivananda: Ethical Teachings, Reshikesh, 2nd edi., 1962.

Tilak, B.G.: Gīta Rahasya or Karmayoga, 2 Vols.-1st Vol. 1995; 2nd Vol. 1936, Poona.

Tiwari, Brij Gopal: Secularism and Materialism in Modern India, Jabalpur.

Thomas P.: Hindu Religion, Custom and Manners.

Thomas P.: Epics Myth and Legends of India Bombay.

Urban: Fundamentals of Ethics, New York, 1956.

Vaidya C. V.: Mahābhārata Mimansa, Poona, Sambat 1979.

Vaidya C. V.: Mahābhārata, a Criticism, Bombay, 2nd edi. 1929.

Vaidya C. V.: Epic India, 1907.

Valavadkar Pandharinath H.: Hindu Social Institutions, Manglore 1939.

Valavadkar Pandharinath H.: Hindu Social Organisation, Bombay, 1954 (Revised edi.).

Vankateswara S.V.: Indian Culture Through the Ages, 2 Vols. London 1928, 1932.

Viswanath S. V.: International Law in Ancient India, 1925.

Vivekanand, Swami: The Complete work of Swamy Vivekanand Vol. IV, 1899.

Vora, D.P.: Evolution of Morals in the Epics, Bombay, 1st edi, 1959.

Williams Monier: Indian Epic poetry, Edinburgh 1863.

Williams Monier: Indian Wisdom, London, 1875.

Williams Monier: Hinduism, London. 1906.

Williams Monier: Religious Thought and Life in India, London 1883.

Williams Monier: Mahābhārata Parichaya, Gita Press, Gorakhpur.

Williams Monier: A Synthesis of the Bhagavadgita, the Shrine of wisdom London 1927.

Williams Monier: History and Culture of Indian people, Vol. II (the age of imperial unity), Bhartiya Vidya Bhawan, Ist edi, 1951.

Williams Monier: Vol. I (The Vedic age), Bhartiya Vidya Bhawan, 4th edi. 1951.

Williams Monier: Sanatan Dharma and advanced text book of Hindu religion and ethics, 2nd edi., Central Hindu College, Benaras,

Williams Monier: The Science of religion, a Sanatana Vaidika dharma; an attempt at an exposition of principles, 2nd edi., Benaras, 1948.

Williams Monier: The Cultural Heritage of India Vol. II, Introduction by Dr. C. P. Ramaswami Aiyar, The Ramkrishna Mission Institute, Calcutta, 2nd edi. 1962.

Younger P. and Younger S.O.: Hinduism Argus Communication, Niles, Illinois, 60468, 1978.

Selected Articles

'Sanatan Dharma or the Moral Life as Conformity to Law', Prof. N. Venkataraman, pub. in the philosophical Quarterly Vol. VIII, No. 1, April 1932.

'The Meaning of Dharma, H.D. Bhattacharya Pub. in Review of Philosophy and Religion, Vol. VII, No. 2, December, 1938.

'Influence: of the Mahābhārata on Hindu Social Life', Shri Shankaracharya (Dr. Kurtakoti) Pub. in Annals of Bhandarkar Oriental Research Institute Journal ABORIJ, Vol. 19, 1938 -39.

'Karma and Reincarnation in the Mahābhārata, H. G. Narahari, ABORIJ, Vol.. XXIV, Part. I-IV.

'The Auhorship of the Mahābhārata', Dr. N. J. Shende, A. B. O. R. I., Vol. XXIV, Part, 1-IV.

'The Dotrine of Karma from the Zoroastrian Point of View', Shams-UL-ULMA, Dr. Javanji Jamshedji Modi in Proceedings and Transactions of the Second Oriental Conference, Calcutta, 1922.

'The Roving Mendicants in the Mahābhārata and Their Teachings', S. N. Gajendragadakar Pub. in Journal of the Asiatic Society of Bombay, Vol. 30, Pt. 1, 1955

'Summum Bonum in the Bhagavadgita', Dr. G. V. Devasthale, Pub. in Bhartiya Vidya, Vol. XIV, 1953.

'Ethic Discourse of Bhīṣma', Krishnalal Mohanlal Jhaveri Pub. in Bhartiya Vidya, Vol. II Part I and II, November, 1940.

'The Hindu Social Philosophy', Pandharinath Valavalkar, Ibid.

'Living Epic', Shravaka, Pub. in The Aryan Path, Vol. 28, January-December, 1957.

'Social Order in old India' (A Symposium), Pub. in the Aryan Path, Vol. X, 1939.

'The Individual in Hindu Polity', V, R. R. Dikshitar, Ibid

'Doctrine of Karma', P. Nagaraja Rao, Pub. in The Aryan Path, Vol. 30. 1959.

'Freewill;, J. N. Ganguli, Ibid.

'The Buddhistic Conception of Dharma', Dr. P. T. Raju, Pub. in Annals of Bhandarkar Oriental Research Institute Vol. 21, 1939-40.

'The Concption of Dharma in the Mahābhārata', Dr. T. M. P. Mahadevan, Pub. in Vedant Kesari, Vol. 37.

'Some Thoughts on Gītā', Swami Siddhenathananda, Pub. In Vedant Kesari, November, 1961.

'The Indian Conception of Values', M. Hiriyanna, Pub. in ABORIJ Vol. 19, 1938-39.

'The Concept of Ancient Indian Warfare', V. R. R. Dikashitar, Pub in The Aryan Path, Vol. 17, 1946.

'Hindu Social Ethics', P. N. Srinevasachari, Pub. in Vedant Kesari, June, 1962.